The Definitive Guide to PSM II

Passing the Professional Scrum Master™ II
exam on your first try.

Moritz Knueppel

Lead in Agile

Training, Consulting, Coaching
lead-in-agile.com
team@lead-in-agile.com

Self-published in February 2023
Second edition
Moritz Knueppel
Hermannstal 89
22119 Hamburg, DE
scrumguide@moritz-knueppel.eu
Copyright © Moritz Knueppel 2023

Table of Contents

Preface 5

Preparations for PSM II 8

Working in complex environments 10

    Why Scrum? 10

    Project plans and project budgets 13

    Measuring Progress 15

    But what about architecture? 20

Scrum Team 22

    Self-Management 24

    Cross-functionality 36

    The Product Owner 38

    Developers 47

    Scrum Master 51

    Changes to the Scrum Team 70

Scrum Events 74

    The Sprint 74

    Sprint Planning 76

    Daily Scrum 84

    Sprint Review 88

    Sprint Retrospective 91

Artifacts 93

    Product Backlog 95

    Sprint Backlog 97

    Increment 99

Scrum Values **102**

Scaling Scrum **105**

    Product Backlog Refinement 108

    Sprint 109

    Sprint Planning 110

    Daily Scrum and Work during the Sprint 111

    Sprint Review 113

    Sprint Retrospective 114

Metrics and Tools **115**

Scrum.org Exams **118**

Image Sources **119**

Disclaimer **119**

Sources **119**

Preface

Scrum offers a way of working that is breaking with seemingly conventional wisdom. Where there used to be strict hierarchies, we are discovering ways for teams to manage their work on their own. Where product development was divided into departments such as planning, requirements engineering, implementation, testing, documentation and release, we are discovering ways to build small teams that are capable of all of this. And perhaps most importantly of all, where projects used to take years, we are now discovering ways to deliver value within a month and often even more quickly than that.

What is this book for?
This book aims to give those already familiar with Scrum a second iteration over the framework. Building on existing knowledge, we dive deeper into the practical application of Scrum, and particularly the role of the Scrum Master. We have an in-depth look at every aspect of the framework, its rules, accountabilities, events, and artifacts and their commitments, and how they all tie together to foster empirical process control.

How is this book structured?
Scrum.org advocates for the idea of Test-Driven-Development (TDD) in software development. This means we first define the tests that our new product increment must fulfill and then work our way there. Analogously, this book will start each section with questions that prepare you for PSM II.
The book will begin by introducing the idea of complex problems and how agile approaches help to address them properly. From there, we will look at each aspect described in the Scrum Guide and discover how the elements foster Scrum's empirical process control. As

this book aims to prepare you for PSM II, particular emphasis will be place on the Scrum Master, and the different stance a Scrum Master should take.

Finally, we will have a look at how Scrum can be scaled, what challenges that brings with it, and how scaled Scrum can be implemented successfully with the help of good Scrum Masters.

What sets this book apart?
There are not a lot of books on the market that aim to prepare you for PSM II. While you can buy books that describe themselves as "question banks" or "exam dumps", they merely prepare you for those specific question they list. The question pool of PSM II is updated and those questions in the books therefore often outdated.

Those books typically don't give you an explanation of the supposedly correct answers, and not too few of them contain severe errors.

If you buy a car, you wish to buy it from a reputable brand at a reputable vendor to be sure of its quality and performance. Equally, you'd want to learn Scrum from a highly knowledgeable source. Regarding Scrum.org's exams, I can say with absolute certainty that there is no PSM II preparation book by an author more familiar with the Scrum.org exams. Why? Because I have taken and passed literally every Scrum.org exam there is.

MORITZ KNÜPPEL
mknueppel94@gmail.com

Moritz's Certifications

Beyond this book
If, after reading this book, you are interested in learning more about Agile Leadership, Scrum, and Kanban, visit my website and book a training course (German or English) for your organization under https://lead-in-agile.com

Preparations for PSM II

Basic information:
- Duration: 90 minutes
- Question: 30; multiple-choice, multi-select, true/false
- Passing score: 85%

After passing your PSM I, taking the PSM II feels like a big step. The questions are of a different nature: rather than being asked to name the timebox of the Sprint Review, you are presented with a small case study of a Sprint Review gone wrong and are asked what the proper path forward is.

Unlike in the PSM I, where each question merely had 45 seconds on average, you can spend up to 3 minutes on each question in your PSM II. Time you will need to properly read and understand the question and answer options, and time you need to evaluate the options based on your knowledge and experience. Often, no answer option is completely false, removing the option you had in PSM I to exclude all clearly false options until you are left with only the correct one(s). In PSM II, however, you are often asked to choose the "best answer" instead, with no option being so obviously false, that they can be excluded outright.

After having taken and passed all of Scrum.org's exams and having guided numerous people through their preparation process for all levels of their PSM exams, I gained an understanding of how the exams are built and how to prepare for them efficiently and effectively.

All the knowledge necessary to pass the PSM II is contained in this book. It contains the distilled essence of what you will need to pass the exam, without lengthy texts about non-essential aspects. Key to passing the exam is to truly understand what is written in this book. The PSM II questions require you to think like a true

Scrum Master, to work with an agile mindset! The tools for this are contained in the text below.

To prepare properly for the exams, read the entire book carefully at least once, ideally twice. Try each time to answer the questions at the beginning of each chapter prior to reading it.

Unlike with the basic exams such as PSM I and PSPO I, there is no open assessment to prepare you for the exam. You may, however, find the 30-question mock quiz on my website useful to get a feeling for the question types. It can be found under: https://scrum-exams.info/psm-ii/

Working in complex environments

Why Scrum?

For a good Scrum Master, it is important to understand the reasons for using agile approaches in general, and Scrum in particular. Unlike what some people think, Scrum is not the right framework for every sort of problem. The Scrum Guide provides us with a clear statement on what sort of problems Scrum is good at addressing.

"Scrum is a lightweight framework that helps people, teams and organizations generate value through adaptive solutions for complex problems."[1]

A useful way to understand what is meant by complex problems is to have a look at how the Cynefin framework[2] differentiates different problem types. In it, we can differentiate complex problems from simple, complicated, and chaotic ones. We will have a look at the first three categories.

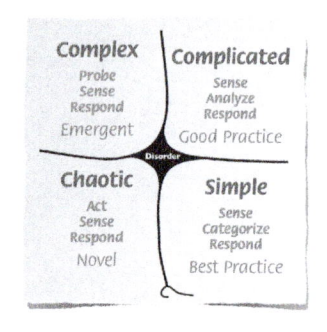

Simple problems are those, where the relationship of cause and effect is constant and easily understandable. Sending a postcard from your vacation is a simple problem. The steps are always the same and easy to understand: buy a postcard, write a few nice sentences on it, put a stamp on it and drop it in a mailbox.

Complicated problems are those, where the relationship of cause and effect is constant as well, but it is not easily understandable. Rather, research, analysis, or expert consultation may be necessary. An example of a complicated problem is fixing an issue on a car. If no whisper fluid is dispensed by your car, it might have several reasons, such as a lack of fluid, a broken pump, an electronics issue, or a clotted hose. To understand the cause, you will need to check several possibilities and eliminate false ones. In short, you conduct an analysis of what is the cause.

When we speak of complex problems - or "complexity" - we mean a problem for which the relationship between action and reaction cannot be known beforehand and is not necessarily constant. Take, for example, the development of a mobile app. The development has finished, testing is done, the app works reliably. Whether or not the market will react positively to it, whether people will be willing to download and even pay for it, is not known. While we can take steps such as market research beforehand, there is no guarantee that releasing our app (action) will lead to a successful acceptance in the marketplace (desired reaction).

In product development, many aspects are complex: market reactions, the interactions within a team, technical problems arising throughout the development effort, and so on. In none of these cases can a definitive statement be made beforehand. Even extensive planning cannot reasonably address complex problems.

In software development, where Scrum has its origin and is to this day most widespread, most product development falls into the categories of complicated and complex. Key parameters that determine whether a problem should be viewed as complicated or complex are:

- the duration of the development: the longer a development effort runs, the more uncertainty is introduced; when the development is done within three months, things will change less significantly than within three years,

- the scope of the development: the larger the development effort, the more uncertainty is introduced; two developers setting up a small webshop has less uncertainty than nine developers building large a customer relationship management system,
- the environment of the development: the more prone the field is to change, the more uncertainty is introduced; building a software product for a government agency, whose requirements change with occasional law changes every few years, has less uncertainty than building a mobile game for end-users, who expect their games to be state-of-the-art with regards to technology.

As a rule of thumb, one can say: most development efforts that take more than a few months and involve more than two developers fall into the category of complex problems.

Under such circumstances, setting up a plan beforehand and strictly implementing it, causes problems. New things are learned along the way and conditions change, making parts of the plan obsolete or less efficient than possible. Thus, frequently adjusting direction based on what is known at the time is the preferred approach for this kind of problem. And this is what is at the heart of Scrum. All elements of Scrum, its roles and rules, its artifacts and their commitments, and its events are set up to maximize this frequent adjustment to what is newly learned. In the Scrum terminology, we refer to this as empirical process control, or empiricism for short, which postulated that we need to work towards creating **transparency** over the things that affect our work, frequently **inspect** those aspects and if deemed necessary, make changes, i.e. **adapt**.

The goal of applying Scrum is to enable those using it to adapt their approaches frequently to allow for the delivery of the possible value under the existing circumstances at the time. In other words, the goal of Scrum is to be agile.

Project plans and project budgets

Question	True	False
Scrum cannot work within environments with fixed budgets.		
It is good practice to frequently inspect budget planning based on value delivered within the Sprints.		

Agile approaches often invoke panic in the minds of those used to classical project management. Under more conventional approaches, we define the customer's expectations, set up a plan for building a product that satisfies those needs, implement the plan, test the resulting product and hand it over to the customer.

A key psychological benefit to such approaches is that we can get a sense of safety from there being a plan. A plan exists that defines how everything will work out. The scope of the product development has been defined, a timeline has been established and the budget has been set.
The problem is that this sense of safety is often a false one, a self-deception. Projects frequently go over time and/or over budget and the resulting product is not always delivering the best possible value to the customer. The more complex a project is, the more likely this is going to happen.

Scope, time, and budget affect each other. In most cases, the determining factor is the budget. Customers want to know the price tag for what they are requesting and make decisions based on financial forecasts. To understand the practical needs of Scrum Teams regarding to budgeting, let's look at two extreme scenarios:

In a perfect world, every budget decision would be made in collaboration and agreement with all key stakeholders. Everybody is always present and has time and motivation enough to come to a consensus on every decision.
In the complete antithesis to this, the customer defines a budget up front and keeps it completely unchanged over time.

The described perfect world is obviously a hypothetical one. No stakeholder will always be present and (want to) be involved in every decision.
The described antithesis, however, is not fictional at all. The idea to combine fixed budgets with Scrum happens rather frequently, usually coming from managers and/or customers with a background in classic project management. And while Scrum is not impossible with fixed budgets, it is made significantly harder.

A good compromise between the two extremes would be to apply Scrum's idea of iterative, incremental development to the budgeting. A few Sprints are financed and the outcomes are continuously inspected by the stakeholders during Sprint Reviews. Since Scrum delivers potentially releasable increments every Sprint, it is possible to frequently assess, whether the customer feels like they are getting enough for their money.
Based on historical trends, forecasts about future costs and deliverables can be made. For those, it must be kept in mind though, they are forecasts and not commitments, i.e. they are potentially subject to changes over time and are not binding.

Solution: False, True

Measuring Progress

Releases and medium-term forecasting

Question	True	False
Scrum allows for accurately measuring project progress.		
The best way to deal with progress measurement is frequent common inspection of the Increment and the Product Backlog.		
Within a Sprint, a Product Owner can ensure that all items in the Sprint Backlog are turned into a potentially releasable Increment.		
A Scrum Master should ensure that stakeholders have transparency by frequently delivering status reports to them.		

A key motivation for setting up project plans is that it gives the impression, that it is
possible to reliably track progress. Oversimplified: if 50% of the tasks outlined in the plan are done within 6 months, we will need another 6 months to finish up the project. In less complex environments, such assumptions may be close to the truth. But the more complex of a problem we are dealing with, the less useful such progress measures become for two key reasons:

1. Environmental changes: we are extrapolating the first 6 months into the future, which only works, if the conditions for the next 6 months are the same - or at least very similar - to those in the first six months.

Important parameters may vary, however. The staffing of the team may change, previously undiscovered bugs may be found, technical debt may accumulate, etc.
2. Changes in priority: we are setting up a plan and implementing it until it is finished. In the meantime, however, new priorities may arise that require a change in the plan. The customer might see a new market opportunity, a competitor may have released a new feature that will need to be copied, legal changes may require different handling of sensitive data, etc.

A project plan may create a sense of control and certainty, though, in complex environments, it would be a false sense. The better thing to do in a complex environment is to ensure that critical information is transparent and frequently inspected and adapted. With regard to progress towards business goals, this means a need for effective work with the Product Backlog and Increment.

The current Increment provides transparency about what has already been implemented. The Product Backlog provides transparency about the current priorities and allows for forecasts (important: not commitments!) about when certain milestones will likely be achieved. Unlike in our example above, this inspection should take place frequently, i.e. during every Sprint, and unlike a fixed project plan, the next steps are determined frequently as well.

This does not ensure, however, that certain planned deadlines will be met. Such a certainty simply does not exist in complex environments. This is a change that many are uncomfortable with, especially those who are used to classic project management approaches. Forecast deadlines may need to be adjusted as more information becomes available. All we can truly ensure is that the Scrum Team is always working on the items that are deemed most valuable at the moment. Forecasts are subject to change and only become more certain the closer we get to their ends.

Explaining these concepts to those not yet familiar with them is one of the key responsibilities of a good Scrum Master. When approached by an important stakeholder inquiring about a progress report, the best course is to show them the Increment, and the Product Backlog and invite them to the next Sprint Review for a discussion with the Product Owner about current forecasts.

Solutions: False, True, False, False

Sprints and short-term forecasting

Complexity not only affects the medium- to long-term planning within a product development effort. Short-term planning is affected as well. The Scrum Team uses its Sprint Planning to create a Sprint Backlog, i.e. a list of Product Backlog items it seeks to implement in order to achieve the Sprint Goal, combined with a plan on how to do the work necessary.

The timeframe that is being planned for (maximum one month) is much shorter than with conventional project plans (several months, often several years). Nonetheless, the same challenge of complexity still applies: a plan can be made, but as conditions change and as more is learned, it may become transparent that the original forecasts were off.

Prior to 2011, the Scrum Guide required the Development Team (which does not exist as a concept anymore since the 2020 Scrum Guide update and is replaced with "Developers") to commit to the Sprint Backlog. In other words, the Development Team made a promise to the Product Owner to implement the items selected in the Sprint Planning. With the 2011 update to the Scrum Guide, this was changed; now the Scrum Guide states that the Developers forecast a Sprint Backlog, i.e. they give their best guess on how much they will be able to achieve and commit to a Sprint Goal.

Somewhat frustrating for those coming from the more conventional project management side, the effect of complexity within a Sprint means that it is very possible for a Scrum Team to not finish all items forecast in the Sprint Planning. Instead, the Developers follow their Sprint Goal and implement those items in the Sprint Backlog whose implementations make achieving the Sprint Goal most likely. There may be Sprints where all items are finished and even more may be pulled during the Sprint. There may, however, also be Sprints in which not all items are finished.

While we may not like this fact, because it contradicts our own need for certainty, plans, and stability, it is an acknowledgment of the reality of planning in a complex environment.

But what about architecture?

Question	True	False
All architecture of a product development should be handled before developing business functionality.		
Architecture is a concern solely of the Developers and are not included in the Product Backlog.		

A frequently arising question, when it comes to developing software products is how architecture is handled within Scrum. Conventional approaches assume that the entire architecture is defined prior to development. While it may not be a bad idea to consider good architectural practices from early Sprints on, designing the whole architecture is not practical and, more importantly, not really possible.

The architecture of a product can be designed somewhat reasonably upfront if we assume that all parameters about the product and its later uses are known and stable. When working in complex environments, this is once again not a given. Priorities may change, requirements may change, technology such as frameworks may change, all affecting architectural decisions.

Therefore, in Scrum, we speak of "emerging architecture". This describes the idea that architecture continually arises when developers implement necessary features, while also paying attention to good architectural practices. Such an approach brings with it the benefit that business value is delivered sooner since it is not required to define the entire architecture before starting the development. This in turn is important for two reasons:

1. delivering value to the customer is the reason for the development effort, and
2. delivering value early allows for gathering feedback from stakeholders early, which allows us to better serve their needs from an early point and avoid wasting resources on e.g. developing features that turn out to be of low value.

In order to assure transparency over architectural work, it can be a good idea to agree within the Scrum Team on architectural conventions, include metrics on this in the Definition of Done, and include necessary architectural work as items in the Product Backlog.

Solutions: False, False

Scrum Team

"The fundamental unit of Scrum is a small team of people, a Scrum Team. The Scrum Team consists of one Scrum Master, one Product Owner, and Developers."[3]

With this sentence, the 2020 Scrum Guide defines the different accountabilities within the Scrum Team. Prior to the 2020 edition, the Scrum Guide used the term "roles" to describe Scrum Master, Product Owner, and - back then - member of the Development Team. This change was intended to emphasize that those are not (necessarily) job titles, but rather functions that need to be taken care of within a Scrum Team. From here on out, I will be referring to these as accountabilities, though for most practical purposes, you may view this as synonymous to the term "roles".

Beyond the accountabilities that must be fulfilled, the Scrum Guide defines two important criteria, that the Scrum Team must (aim to) meet: self-management and cross-functionality.
Self-management describes the idea that the Scrum Team is itself deciding who does what and when.
Cross-functionality describes the idea that the skill set present within the team must be sufficient to create valuable Increments every Sprint.

These two criteria create an implicit requirement regarding the size of a Scrum Team. Since the 2020 Scrum Guide, there is no more strict rule on how many members a team may have. Instead, the teams have to decide for themselves, how many members make sense, keeping in mind that
- larger teams are more complex and thus make self-management harder
- smaller teams can create less value and are thus less cross-functional.

A guideline given by the Scrum Guide is "typically 10 or fewer", though this is not to be understood as a static rule.

In the following sections, we will look at self-management, cross-functionality, each accountability (with a special focus on that of the Scrum Master), and how changes to the Scrum Team should be dealt with.

Self-Management

The term self-management was newly introduced in the 2020 Scrum Guide update. Prior to its publication, Scrum Teams were described as self-organizing. To understand the motivation for this change, let's look at the respective Scrum Guide definitions:

2017 Scrum Guide: "Self-organizing teams choose how best to accomplish their work, rather than being directed by others outside the team."[4]

2020 Scrum Guide: "[Scrum Teams] ... also self-managing, meaning they internally decide who does what, when, and how."[5]

The 2017 definition contains no information on who defines what is to be worked on. Under this, the team decides the how and the when, but not necessarily the what. However, the 2017 Scrum Guide also includes the provisions that the work of the Development Team (now: Developers) must originate from the Product Backlog, which is maintained by a Product Owner, who is part of the Scrum Team.

The change from self-organizing to self-managing strengthens the already existing idea that Scrum Teams determine not just how to do their work and when, but also what that work is.

To look at self-management in detail, we will discuss how Scrum fosters self-management, what practical criteria we can use to determine whether a team is self-managing or not, and look at the benefits of self-managing teams over traditionally managed teams.

How Scrum fosters self-management

Question	True	False
Self-managing teams do not have managers, as they are self-managing.		
Scrum supports self-management through eliminating management positions.		
Scrum supports self-management through changing the understanding of the jobs of management towards a team.		
Scrum supports self-management through Sprint Retrospectives.		
Delivering valuable increments is an important metric of self-management.		
While time-boxing is sometimes necessary, it can impede a team's ability to self-manage.		

We can split the necessities for self-management into two broad categories:

- On the one hand, it is necessary for teams to be allowed to self-manage. While Scrum does not mandate the removal of managers, it does implicitly require a change in management style, from traditional management towards agile leadership. A team cannot be truly self-managing if a manager exists who is empowered by the organization to give orders to the team and potentially micro-manage them.

- On the other hand, it is necessary for teams to be capable of self-management. Simply having management not intervene in the internal affairs of a team does not lead to self-management. The responsibilities previously fulfilled by a manager must now be taken care of by the team itself, complicated by the fact that decisions must now be taken commonly in some form of consensus, rather than by one person with hierarchical power.

Ensuring that self-management is allowed is one of the key responsibilities of a Scrum Master, particularly during a transition from a traditional management structure towards a Scrum environment. It is the job of the Scrum Master to ensure that the management understands the requirements and benefits of self-management and its necessity for the success of a Scrum Team. Furthermore, it is important for a Scrum Master to assist existing management in their transition towards a different management style.
A common misconception is that Scrum seeks to eliminate management positions. Rather, Scrum may necessitate a change in the understanding and practice of management and leadership. A good "manager" in a Scrum environment does not stand in the way of their team's self-management, but actively fosters it by making sure the team has all the resources it needs to succeed.

As each environment is different. Therefore, the approaches of an individual Scrum Master must also be different to overcome the challenge of working towards the empowerment of their teams. For this work, however, it is helpful to have a deeper understanding of the stances of a Scrum Master, which will be discussed in a later chapter.

In Scrum, a team's ability for self-management is not to be understood as an on-or-off thing, but rather a desirable end-goal towards which the teams should strive. The key manner in which this is achieved is through empirical process control, i.e. transparency, inspection, and adaptation. Scrum provides the following aspects that aid in teams improving their self-management capabilities:

- Sprint Retrospectives: they provide a platform to inspect the current level of self-management capabilities within a team and to take steps to adapt.

- Incremental development: latest by the end of a Sprint, a new valuable, Done Increment must have been created. Whether or not a team is able to continually deliver Increments that meet their Sprint Goals is a key indicator for the team's ability to self-manage. Observing this indicator creates the necessary transparency for subsequent inspection and adaptation.

- Time-boxing: all events within a Sprint and the Sprint itself are time-boxed. Clearly limiting the time an activity is allowed to take ensures that those involved are required to focus on the most important aspects. This strengthens the Scrum Value of focus, it is in itself a tool to push people towards self-management and provides yet another metric on the team's ability to self-manage. A team that is not able to keep time-boxes still has work to do towards achieving self-management.

- The Scrum Master: "[c]oaching the team members in self-management ..." is the first service of a Scrum Master towards a Scrum Team that is listed in the Scrum Guide.[6] Transitioning towards self-management is not an easy task and thus the Scrum Guide mandates every Scrum Team to have a Scrum Master, whose responsibilities include helping along with this transition. The tools a Scrum Master can use for this will be discussed in the chapter on the Scrum Master and their stances.

Solutions: False, False, True, True, True, False

Criteria of self-managing teams

Question	True	False
The Product Owner has the final say on what the Scrum Team works on.		
Nobody but the Scrum Team may take part in the Spring Planning.		
Nobody but the Scrum Team may decide on the Sprint Goal.		
The Product Owner decides how many Product Backlog items are pulled into the Sprint Backlog.		
The Sprint Backlog, once established, is implemented strictly to plan.		
All information necessary to implement the Product Backlog items in the Sprint Backlog are discussed during the Sprint Planning. Therefore, there is no need for communication between Developers and Product Owner during the Sprint.		
The Developers may remove Product Backlog items if deemed necessary, as they own the Sprint Backlog.		
The Developers are accountable for the outcome of the Sprint.		
If the Sprint fails due to a lack of proper testing, not just the tester is accountable for the failure, but the whole Scrum Team.		

For Scrum Masters, one key responsibility is coaching the Scrum Team members towards self-management. For this, we take an empirical approach, meaning that we

continually inspect the self-management abilities of the team and make subsequent adjustments in our actions.
To be able to properly inspect the degree to which a team is already self-managing, it is necessary to understand what to look for. We will examine the key criteria along the timeline from a customer requirement to a delivered Increment. At every stage, remember that both empowerment and capability need to be given: the Scrum Team must be allowed to take the mentioned steps and have the necessary skills, tools, and mindset to be able to actually do it.

Product Owner Autonomy
The Scrum Guide defines that the Product Owner holds the final authority on what the Scrum Team works on. They are the ones to decide what goes into the Product Backlog and what does not, and how the items are ordered inside the Product Backlog at any given time. For a truly self-managing Scrum Team, the Product Owner's decisions must be respected by everybody, including management.
Thus, in a self-managing Scrum Team, a customer requirement is evaluated by the Product Owner and placed into the Product Backlog as a Product Backlog Item (PBI) according to their assessment.

Building a Sprint Backlog
The Scrum Team uses the Sprint Planning to build their Sprint Backlog. In this meeting, the Scrum Team may decide to add externals that help them get a better understanding of certain items or their implementation. However, the Scrum Team maintains the final authority to define the Sprint Goal and the Developers the final authority on the creation of the Sprint Backlog.
The Product Owner defines what items are to be worked upon, the Developers decide on how many items they believe to be able to achieve and how to implement them. The Scrum Team collectively defines the Sprint Goal that provides direction for the Sprint.

Thus, in a self-managing Scrum Team, our customer PBI is pulled into the Sprint according to the Scrum Team's assessment, and its implementation is planned by the Developers according to their own assessment.

Inspecting and adapting the Sprint Backlog
Every workday, the progress towards the Sprint Goal is inspected and subsequently, the plan on how to achieve it may be adapted. This work is done autonomously by the Developers. Neither the Product Owner, nor Scrum Master, nor outsiders may order the Developers to act in a certain way.
Thus, in a self-managing Scrum Team, the work necessary for our customer PBI may be re-planned and re-prioritized with respect to the Sprint Goal.

Gathering necessary information
The Developers may not have all the necessary information to implement a particular PBI. As we work in a complex environment, even careful refinement and planning cannot always avoid this. A self-managing Scrum Team is capable of resolving this on its own.
Thus, in a self-managing Scrum Team, Developers and Product Owner may need to collaborate to clarify aspects of our customer PBI.

Adjusting the scope of the Sprint Backlog
If during the Sprint it is determined that the Developers will not be able to implement all items in the Sprint Backlog, this information is made transparent as soon as possible. The Developers work with the Product Owner to evaluate the current situation and determine which items
- to remove from the Sprint Backlog while keeping the Sprint Goal achievable.

Thus, in a self-managing Scrum Team, Developers and Product Owner may determine to remove our customer PBI from the Sprint Backlog, while keeping the Sprint Goal intact.

Collective accountability for the outcome
Once the Sprint is finished, the resulting Increment is inspected in the Sprint Review. The entire Scrum Team is accountable for the outcome, regardless of how the work was divided internally. This is one key reason for there being no titles among the Developers, even if they may have different expertise.
The Product Owner and Scrum Master share the accountability with the Developers for the same reason. Scrum is focused on producing results; if a Scrum Team does not produce good results, the entire team owns that failure and must collectively take steps to adjust their course.
Thus, in a self-managing Scrum Team, the whole team owns the accountability for delivering a valuable Increment, and no sub-teams or titles exist among the Developers.

Internal conflict resolution
Where ever two or more people are working together, conflict is bound to arise eventually. This is normal and perfectly healthy within a team. A commonly cited model is the Tuckman Model, which outlines that every team undergoes the phases of
- forming - the team is first gathered and the people get to know each other,
- storming - as the collaboration goes on, first conflicts arise,
- norming - the team manages to resolve its conflict and defines its way of working together peacefully,
- performing - the team has reached a state where internal conflicts are no longer affecting the productivity of the team.

A team undergoes such a process frequently and should be able to make the step from storming to norming on its own. Otherwise, the team lacks some necessary tools or skills to do so.
This, a self-managing team has the ability to resolve normal conflicts internally and does not require outside help.

A Scrum Master should continually observe these criteria to evaluate the extent to which their team is already self-managing and to derive further necessary actions to support the team towards self-management.

Solutions: True, False, True, False, False, False, False, False, True

Benefits of self-managing teams

Question	True	False
Self-management is there to eliminate all management positions.		
Self-managing teams are typically more creative than managed teams.		

Unlike what some people may believe, the idea of self-managing teams is not in place due to an inherent, ethical disapproval of hierarchies and management. Rather, like all aspects in Scrum, it is there to improve the applicability of empirical process control.

Empirical process control consists of three pillars: transparency, inspection, and adaptation. Self-managing teams are generally better with regards to all three of these.

Self-managing teams are much closer to the relevant information. A Developer in a software product development knows much more about the relevant source code, its architecture, bugs, and technical debts than a project manager, who may not even have a technical background. A Product Owner knows more about the needs of their stakeholders than somebody two hierarchy levels removed, who has never met a single stakeholder personally. While these examples are a bit overdrawn, they illustrate the principle that those closest to the work usually have the highest degree of information.

Due to the higher degree of transparency, self-managing teams are better at inspection. During the Daily Scrum, the Developers inspect the Sprint Backlog. It is the plan they created and the work they have been doing, are doing and will be doing. It's much more efficient for them to identify problems or upcoming risks than for somebody from the outside to do so.

Adaptation is both more efficient and more effective in a self-managing team. This is partly due to the better inspection, which allows for a better understanding of the issue and a subsequently better understanding of possible actions to take.
Beyond that, those defining the changes and those practically owning the consequences of the changes are identical. A team that agrees to try a new approach together will commit to this much more than a team that is being told to try the same approach by a manager.
Lastly, within the relative safety of a Scrum Team, members will feel more open to express ideas of possible adaptations. As more possibilities are discussed and the team has the courage to try new paths, better and more creative adaptations are possible.

The goal of self-managing teams is not to get rid of management per se. Neither is the goal to eventually get rid of having a Scrum Master, as some people falsely believe. The intention of the Scrum Guide's idea of self-managing teams is very clearly formulated in its 2017 edition. In it, it is stated that "[t]he team model in Scrum is designed to optimize flexibility, creativity, and productivity".[7]

Solutions: False, True

The 100 Developer Problem

One of the most common examples for the application of self-management is a hypothetical scenario drawn up by Scrum's co-creator Ken Schwaber in a 2012 blog post.[8] He raises the question of what the best way to organize 100 developers into Scrum Teams would be.

A conventional approach would now utilize tools like a skill matrix, request information from previous tech leads, or even set up teams along the lines of previously existing teams as it is thought that those people are compatible with each other. Schwaber argues, however, that the best way to organize those 100 developers is not organize them at all, but to let them self-organize.

Self-management needs clear boundaries and transparency. In this example, the Product Owner would present the product vision and other elements relevant to the development. The Scrum Master would organize and facilitate the event. Beyond that, Schwaber argues for what he calls "bottom-up intelligence", noting that the best decision will be reached by those with the most information relevant to the decision, which in this case are the developers.

Many organizations would struggle to allow for such an event to take place, citing an array of concerns. For positive examples as well as a guideline for organizing such self-selection workshops, I recommend you have a look at the book *Creating Great Teams: How Self-Selection Lets People Excel*.[9]

This example illustrates that self-management is not merely an attribute of an individual team, but a mindset that must spread throughout the entire organization if a Scrum implementation is to be maximally effective.

Cross-functionality

Question	True	False
In a cross-functional team, all the skills necessary to build an Increment are present.		
Every Developer on a cross-functional Scrum Team has all the necessary skills to turn any Product Backlog item into an Increment.		

The term "cross-functionality" describes the idea the team is capable of delivering a valuable, Done, potentially releasable Increment by the end of the Sprint. This requirement has a significant impact on the setup of a Scrum Team. In an environment with only one Scrum Team - as opposed to a scaled scrum environment - the Scrum Team must be capable of turning Product Backlog items into working Increments of the product.

The range of skill varies strongly between different domains and even between individual products in the same domain. When developing a marketing campaign using Scrum, the skills necessary might be design, PR, and legal expertise. In a product development in the software domain, however, it might be frontend, backend, database, and testing expertise.

It is crucial for the success of a Scrum Team to continually inspect whether it has all the abilities necessary to deliver valuable Increments without needing outside support. If it is found that the team cannot deliver such valuable increments on its own, necessary adaptation steps must be taken, i.e. the team must determine how to acquire the abilities, for example, either by learning new skills or adding people with expertise to the team.

It is often - falsely - assumed, that every Developer must possess all the skills necessary for turning any Product Backlog item into an Increment. This is merely a myth. The determination of whether or a Scrum Team is cross-functional is based upon whether the entire team collectively has the necessary abilities. Often it can be useful for everybody on the team to have a broad skill set, but this may not always be achievable and is not required.

In a software development environment, for example, not everybody has to know frontend, backend, databases, and testing. Working towards Developers who have at least a decent skill level in each, may, however, make coordination between the Developers easier and make the team as a whole more flexible. The determination of whether this is worth the effort and, if so, how this is to be achieved, is a determination, which the self-managing Scrum Team makes for itself.

Solutions: True, False

The Product Owner

The Product Owner is a position that is frequently misunderstood, even in organizations that claim themselves to be proficient in applying Scrum.

To better understand the real job of a Product Owner, we'll look at the relationships of a Product Owner with

- their product and the Product Backlog
- their Scrum Team
- those with an active interest in the product, i.e. the stakeholders

Product Owner, Product and Product Backlog

Question	True	False
One product can have multiple Product Owners.		
Defining one Product Owner per product ensures clarify over who makes the final decisions over the Product Backlog.		
The Product Owner's role is that of a value-maximizer.		
The key way to optimise the value delivered is by assigning tasks to individual developers.		
To order the Product Backlog, the Product Owner must consult Return-on-Invest (ROI), current burn-up charts and the Gantt charts of the project.		
The Product Owner is responsible for writing User Stories.		
Product Backlog management is the responsibility of the Product Owner and cannot be delegated to somebody else.		
The Product Owner is accountable for the order of the items in the Product Backlog.		

When talking about the relationship between Product Owner, Product Backlog, and product, there are a few simple rules to remember:

Product and Product Backlog
The Product Backlog serves the purpose of gathering all relevant information about the possible next steps of a product. Rather than having a variety of different

(sub-)plans and documents in different places with possibly different accessibility, the Product Backlog in Scrum unifies all relevant information in one place. By making this information accessible to the Scrum Team and relevant stakeholders, the Product Owner creates transparency.

Having multiple Product Backlogs for one product would lower transparency since not all information could be found in one place.

At the same time, maintaining one Product Backlog for multiple products would place different information, possibly relevant to different stakeholders, into the same place that does not belong together. This would make the Product Backlog more difficult to understand and thus less transparent.

Thus, the rule is: *one Product Backlog per product and one product per Product Backlog.*

Product Owner and Product Backlog

The Product Owner is defined in the Scrum Guide as a single person, who holds the final authority on the decisions about the Product Backlog. Sometimes, you may see things like "Product Owner groups" or "Product Owner councils", which aim to replace the idea of a single Product Owner with a group of people. This is a violation of the ideas of Scrum.

The Product Owner is defined as a single person because this ensures that there is exactly one person who takes the decisions regarding the Product Backlog. Multiple Product Owner may give different opinions to stakeholders and their own Scrum Team or will have the need to come to an agreement on every single decision. The former will inevitably lead to misunderstandings and unclarity and thereby reduce transparency, the latter would slow down decision-making processes and lower flexibility.

While there may be groups supporting and advising the Product Owner, there has to be only one person finally accountable for the Product Backlog in Scrum and that is the one, single Product Owner.

There is, however, no rule that speaks against the idea of a person being the Product Owner accountable for multiple Product Backlogs (of multiple products) per se. While the workload should be carefully considered and sufficient availability towards Developers and stakeholders must be ensured, one person can, in principle, be the Product Owner accountable for multiple Product Backlogs.

Thus, the rule is: *one Product Owner per Product Backlog, but potentially multiple Product Backlogs for multiple products per Product Owner.*

Product Owner and Product Backlog and Product
By joining the two previous rules together, it becomes clear that one person can be the Product Owner of either
- one product and therefore one Product Backlog
- multiple products and therefore multiple Product Backlogs

Thus, the rule is:
A Product has exactly one Product Backlog and exactly one Product Owner. But a Product Owner may have multiple products, each with exactly one Product Backlog.

Product Backlog Management
The primary accountability of the Product Owner is to maximize the value resulting from the work done by the Scrum Team. To achieve this, the Product Owner's most important tool is the Product Backlog, which consists of two elements: the current Product Goal and Product Backlog items.

The ordering of the Product Backlog reflects the current priorities: higher-ranked items will be worked on sooner than lower-ranked ones.

The metrics used to decide on the order of items in the Product Backlog are left to the Product Owner. In general, Scrum is non-prescriptive regarding tools, methods, and approaches to be employed by the Product Owner. This applies as well to the format of Product Backlog items. While it may be a good idea to employ the format of user stories, this is not obligatory and not part of Scrum.

Something that is often surprising to people is the fact that even this core activity can be delegated to others. To understand this, we need to understand the Scrum Guide's distinction between accountability and responsibility. Slightly simplified, the difference can be explained as such:

The term "responsibility" describes whose job it is to a specific activity, who has been assigned the task to work on it. Meanwhile, the term "accountability" describes who is liable for the outcome of the activity, who would be "to blame" if the specific activity is not finished or does not turn out well.

Imagine you invite friends over for dinner and you let your 10-year-old child help you by cooking the pasta. It is the child's job to cook the pasta, but if the pasta ends up overcooked, your friends will not put the blame on your 10-year-old child but on you. In this example, cooking the pasta was the child's responsibility but your accountability.

A Product Owner may delegate the responsibility of managing the Product Backlog, e.g. by ordering the items within it, to somebody else. The Product Owner does, however, remain accountable for the order of the Product Backlog and for the increments that are created on the basis of it.

Solutions: False, True, True, False, False, False, False, True

Product Owner and Scrum Team

Question	True	False
The Product Owner is virtually identical to a project manager.		
The Product Owner must attend all Scrum Events.		
The Product Owner only has contact with the Developers during Sprint Planning, Sprint Review and Sprint Retrospective.		

The Product Owner is a fellow member of the Scrum Team. While they have a different set of accountabilities from the Developers, the Product Owner is not in a hierarchical relationship with the Developers. The Product Owner is not the boss of the Developers, despite this often being the case in the real world, when the Product Owner job is falsely equated with that of a project manager. The Scrum Guide imagines a team of equals, which fosters the division of what is important to be built (Product Owner) and how that implementation should take place (Developers).

As a peer Scrum Team member, the Product Owner participates in those Scrum Events relevant to them:

In the Sprint Planning, they propose how the next Sprint could be used to increase value, collaborate with the Developers to decide upon which Product Backlog items are pulled into the Sprint Backlog, and work with Scrum Master and Developers to craft a Sprint Goal.
In the Sprint Review, the Product Owner gathers feedback from the attending stakeholders and subsequently makes adaptations to the Product Backlog.

In the Sprint Retro, they participate alongside the other Scrum Team members to figure out ways to improve the value delivered by the Scrum Team.

Unless the Product Owner is also a Developer at the same time, something which is not highly common, but also not forbidden in Scrum, they do not have to attend the Daily Scrum. They may voluntarily attend, though they do not participate.

Outside of the Scrum Events, the Product Owner should be available to the Developers. As the Sprint progresses, more is learned and therefore new questions may arise that need inputs from the Product Owner. Typical examples are clarifications of requirements, decisions on technical trade-offs, and changes to the scope of the Sprint Backlog if it is determined that not all items in the Sprint Backlog will be achieved.

Solutions: False, False, False

Product Owner and stakeholders

Question	True	False
A key activity of a Product Owner is to engage with stakeholders during the Sprint.		
The most important stakeholder to satisfy is the customer.		
Satisfaction of the customers must be measured at least on a monthly basis.		

In order to maximize the value delivered by the Scrum Team's work, the Product Owner must have an understanding of what constitutes value. A product aims to deliver functionality to its users and in the process becomes relevant to a number of different individuals or groups. Those who are impacted by the success or failure of the product development are referred to as stakeholders.

To understand what next step would maximize the value delivered by the product, the Product Owner must have a good grasp of who the stakeholders are, what their respective interests, are and often how to balance these various interests against each other. Therefore, one of the key activities of a Product Owner besides attending the relevant Scrum Events and working with the Developers is to engage with the stakeholders.

How this stakeholder engagement happens varies widely between different stakeholders and different products.
Two key stakeholders are always the customer and the user. A user is a person using the product, a customer the one paying for it. These two stakeholders may be identical or different. When you buy a video game for yourself, you are both the customer and user. However, if

the company you work for decides to use s new time-tracking software product and buys a license for it, the company is the customer and you are one of the users.

To understand how differences in products affect how a Product Owner engages with stakeholders, let's take an example of the most important stakeholder: the users. We can understand that engaging with the 400,000 users of a mobile app requires a different approach than engaging with the 10 users of a highly customized accounting software. Different techniques and approaches have to be used depending on the circumstances. Determining and applying the right tools and methods is a key part of Product Ownership.

The Product Owner must also have an eye on customer satisfaction, as the paying customer is the one keeping the operation running and is crucial in determining what constitutes value. Thus, it is vital for a Product Owner to frequently measure the satisfaction of the product's customers. The meaning of "frequently" depends, again, on the context. With our previously mentioned mobile app, we may want to get feedback every day, while in the case of the accounting software, it may be sufficient to inquire every month or even less often.

Solutions: True, True, False

Developers

Question	True	False
The Developers are responsible for creating a plan on how to do the work of the upcoming Sprint.		
If estimates are used, the Developers are the only ones to provide them.		
The Scrum Team is responsible for managing the progress of work during the Sprint.		
The Developers update the Sprint Backlog exactly once a day during the Daily Scrum. This ensures transparency over the decisions made.		
The Developers are responsible for re-planning the remaining work of the Sprint if necessary.		
The Developers may not add or remove items from the Sprint Backlog on their own.		

The Developers are those members of the Scrum Team who turn Product Backlog items into working Increments. Prior to the 2020 Scrum Guide release, we spoke of a "Development Team" and subsequently "members of a Development Team", rather than simply of "Developers". The change is an arguably minor one in practice and was merely put in place to strengthen the notion that there are sub-entities within a Scrum Team. The Scrum Team is one team, everybody is supposed to be a team with each other equally.

The specific work done by the Developers is highly dependent on the individual product development. While "Developers" may invoke the idea of a software developer, i.e. somebody who builds software products, the term is supposed to refer to everybody who is developing any product in a Scrum environment. As mentioned in the section on cross-functionality, developing a new marketing campaign might mean that the "Developers" are designers, PR professionals, and legal counsel.

Among Developers there can be differences in specializations, such as the ones mentioned above. However, the accountability of delivering a Done increment is shared by all Developers and the Scrum Team as a whole. If, for example, the new increment of a marketing campaign was not finished due to problems with the design, we recognize this as a common problem, not something to blame on the designer. The entire team, Developers and possibly Product Owner and Scrum Master as well, has not planned and inspected and adapted properly throughout the Sprint to anticipate and mitigate this issue.

The Scrum Guide defines four specific accountabilities for the Developers, which we will look at in detail:

Creating a plan for the Sprint, the Sprint Backlog
During the Sprint Planning, the Scrum Team decides upon a Sprint Goal and Product Backlog items to achieve the Sprint Goal. The Developers are responsible for determining and communicating a forecast of how much work they believe is achievable in the Sprint.

The specific method for doing this is left up to the team. A commonly used tool is that of estimations, which used to be mandatory until the 2017 Scrum Guide. As the Developers have the best understanding of the work required to implement Product Backlog items, the forecast is only created by the Developers. Subsequently, if estimations are used, the Developers are the only ones to make estimations.

The Developers create an initial plan for how to achieve the work on the selected Product Backlog items.

Instilling quality by adhering to a Definition of Done
The Definition of Done, often abbreviated as "DoD", serves as the common quality standard and is used to determine when an increment is "Done". It can be seen as an agreement between the Scrum Team and the stakeholders, but also as an agreement within the Scrum Team, particularly between the Developers and the Product Owner.
The Developers are required to adhere to the Definition of Done to ensure transparency of the Increment. We will be looking at the Definition of Done, its uses, and importance in a later chapter.

Adapting their plan each day toward the Sprint Goal
The Developers are the ones who create the plan on achieving the Sprint Goal. As the Sprint goes on and more is learned, this plan might need to change and it is the job of the Developers to manage the progress of work, inspect the Sprint Backlog and make adaptations to the existing plan.

A key opportunity to do this is the Daily Scrum. It is, however, not the only time when the Sprint Backlog may be updated. The Daily Scrum defines the minimum frequency to do so, if it is determined by the Developers that updates between Daily Scrums are necessary and beneficial, they should be done.

One possible outcome of an inspection might be the recognition that there are too many items in the current Sprint Backlog and that not all will be implementable in the current Sprint. The subsequent adaptation consists of the Developers creating transparency about this to the Product Owner. The Developers and Product Owner then collaborate to redefine the scope of individual items or to remove individual items from the Sprint Backlog, while keeping the Sprint Goal intact and achievable.

The details of how to implement the items in the Sprint Backlog are left to the Developers. The content of the Sprint Backlog, however, can only be changed in collaboration with the Product Owner. This includes both the removal of items discussed above, as well as the addition of items. People from outside the Scrum Team may not force the addition of items into the Sprint Backlog. If supposedly important items arise, those people are required to discuss their needs with the Scrum Team, which then decides on whether or not to add the item to the current Sprint Backlog.

Holding each other accountable as professionals
This accountability is a key necessity for self-management. The Scrum Team as a whole is self-managing and, with regard to the development, the Developers as a group are self-managing. In order for this to work, the Developers need to collaborate, support each other, drive each other forward but also hold each other accountable, for example for the quality of their work. In Scrum, this is seen as a manifestation of the value of respect, which will be discussed in a later chapter.

Solutions: True, True, False, False, True, True

Scrum Master

The third accountability on the Scrum Team is the Scrum Master. Beyond a deep understanding of Scrum itself, a good Scrum Master should be aware of their position relative to the team. Different aspects of the work of a Scrum Master require different approaches. To better understand these, we will be looking at "The 8 Stances of a Scrum Master", a white paper published by Professional Scrum Trainer Barry Overeem.[10]

As the title implies, in his whitepaper, Overeem lays out 8 stances that a good Scrum Master should be aware of and take when appropriate. In the following sections, we will inspect each stance in detail.

Servant Leader

Question	True	False
A Servant Leader places their own needs first.		
A Servant Leader empowers the people they work with.		
Coaching others is one activity of a Servant Leader.		
The stance of the Facilitator is clearly distinct from the Servant Leader.		
Impediment removal is a key activity of Servant Leaders.		

The Scrum Master used to be described in the Scrum Guide as a servant leader. With the 2020 Scrum Guide update, this was changed to "true leader".[11] The stance remains titled "Servant Leader", however. A Servant Leader is described as someone who prioritizes the needs of their fellow team members and leads through empowering others to reach their potential.

We can see this in many aspects of the Scrum Master. While the Product Owner determines the best path for value delivery and the Developers create value by producing increments, the Scrum Master's accountabilities are only indirectly related to value delivery.

It is their job to help the Product Owner and Developers better understand Scrum and (the need for) empirical work and to help the organization and stakeholders better understand how to support the needs of the Scrum Team. In this sense, the Scrum Master leads the team towards greater success by serving their team, hence "Servant Leader".

Another typical example of servant leadership is ensuring that the Scrum Events "take place and are positive, productive, and kept within the timebox"[12]. How exactly this is done can vary between teams and may require further stances, such as the Facilitator and the Coach, which we will be looking at next.

Lastly, a big part of empowering a team is to remove structural obstacles in their way. We refer to this as impediment removal. This aspect is so crucial, that Overeem defined an entire stance, that of the Impediment Remover, for this.

Solutions: False, True, True, False, True

Facilitator

Question	True	False
A good Scrum Master facilitates all discussions in a Scrum Team to ensure maximum efficiency.		
A Scrum Master can help resolve disagreements within the team by facilitating discussions.		
The Scrum Master should be involved in all discussions to ensure they can intervene if necessary.		

Facilitating discussions and events is one of the key tools of a Scrum Master. While in a perfect world, all conversations would be perfectly constructive, goal-oriented, and productive, Scrum recognizes that in the real world, this is not the case. Therefore, the Scrum Master takes up the responsibility to ensure effective discussions and events. The particular tactics used depend on the individual case, though common elements are:

- setting the proper environment, for example: a heated discussion is better kept in a separate room in a smaller circle;
- ensuring preparation: making sure everybody is properly prepared for the event to maximize efficiency;
- ensuring the purpose of the discussion is understood by everybody and that all discussion focusses towards fulfilling that purpose;
- moderating discussions: defining a mode of discussion with a neutral moderator can be helpful when the group is large and/or sides of an argument are beginning to form.

It is important to distinguish between the stance of the Facilitator with the misunderstood stance of the Super Hero. A Scrum Master should not solve every little problem of the team and should not suppress conflict. Not every discussion within the team should be facilitated by the Scrum Master.

A key element of self-management, towards which the Scrum Master should guide their team, is to find solutions to problems and resolve conflicts on their own. The Facilitator stance should become active when the Scrum Master determines that non-intervention at this point would create larger problems.

If, for example, there is disagreement about the meaning of items in the Definition of Done, the careful approach of a Scrum Master would be to let the Developers figure it out for themselves. Only when it becomes clear, that the problem won't be resolved on its own, does the Scrum Master intervene and facilitate a productive discussion on the matter. Following this, the Scrum Master needs to take steps to increase the Developer's ability to resolve similar cases in the future by, for example, coaching them on conflict resolution.

There is a risk of creating a strong dependence of the team on the facilitation. In the worst-case scenario, the Scrum Master becomes somewhat of an information bottleneck, because all information exchanges involve the Scrum Master. This is to be avoided! What we aim at is as much direct communication as possible.

Solutions: False, True, False

Coach

Question	True	False
The Scrum Master coaches the Product Owner regarding their interactions with people. Topics like Product Backlog management are the sole accountability of the Product Owner and are hence not a subject of coaching.		
The Scrum Master can support the Product Owner by coaching them towards more useful interactions with the Developers.		
The Scrum Master can support the Developers by coaching them in conflict management and conflict resolution.		
When the Developers try to alter key parameters of the Daily Scrum, the Scrum Master orders them to stick to the rules of Scrum.		
One key topic of coaching for a Scrum Master is timeboxing.		
The Scrum Master coaches their Scrum Team. Coaching beyond the scope of their team is the responsibility of an Agile Coach.		

A crucial stance of a Scrum Master is that of the Coach. To understand this, let's look at a definition of the term "coaching":

"Coaching refers to guidance and feedback about specific knowledge, skills, and abilities involved in a task"[13]

In practice, coaching can take many forms and the specific approaches should be adjusted to the needs of the individual coachees. Some coachees may require a lot of empathy as they are struggling with adjusting themselves to Scrum. Others may need a lot of constructive, critical feedback to allow them to better adjust to changing conditions. Yet others may merely need somebody to ask a few good questions that kickstart a thinking process.

The Scrum Master is a coach towards individuals, teams, and organizations. We will look at individual coaching relations with the Product Owner and the Developers, the Scrum Team as a whole, and the organization.

Product Owner
The two key interactions of the Product Owner are with the stakeholders and with the Developers.
The Scrum Master can coach the Product Owner towards a better understanding of empirical product development, effective Product Backlog management, and useful ways of gathering stakeholder feedback.
In the interactions of the Product Owner and Developers, the Scrum Master can coach the Product Owner towards more effective collaboration by making them understand what kind of needs the Developers have and what kind of input they require.

Developers
The Developers primarily interact with each other and with the Product Owner.
As the Developers are a group, it is especially important for the Scrum Master to coach the Developers on conflict management and resolution. Conflicts are bound to occur, but having the skills to constructively address them can make the difference between a short-lived disagreement and a major fight.
As the Developers are the owners of the Daily Scrum, it is important for the Scrum Master to coach the

Developers regarding the Daily Scrum. The Developers need to understand the purpose of the event and that they are the ones responsible for organizing, conducting, and improving it within the framework of Scrum. When Developers seek to alter core parameters of the Daily Scrum, such as its frequency and attendance, it is especially important for the Scrum Master to spark discussions about the possible consequences of those changes and why they will decrease the effectiveness of the Scrum Team as a whole. The Scrum Master leads with good arguments, not with power.

Scrum Team
The Scrum Master must ensure that the whole Scrum Team understands the purpose of the Scrum Events and makes full use of them. Especially the Sprint Review and the Sprint Retrospective are often not used to their fullest possible extent, which is where the Scrum Master must coach their fellow team members.
Another common point that leads to discussions within the Scrum Team is the Definition of Done. Here, the Scrum Master must coach the Scrum Team towards a proper understanding of the use of the Definition of Done in creating transparency of the Increment.
Lastly, a common coaching topic within a Scrum Team is the issue of timeboxing. Humans seem to have a tendency to extend timeboxes wherever possible. It is the Scrum Master's responsibility to make sure everybody understands the value provided by timeboxing and helps them better stick to the set timeboxes by making their meetings more efficient.

The Organization
Scrum Teams do not operate in a vacuum. They are usually embedded in a larger organization, often companies, that consist of different departments and hierarchy levels. The Scrum Master coaches those in the organization which interact with the Scrum Team on what

interactions are helpful and which ones are not. It must be ensured that those around the Scrum Team understand the reason for using Scrum and how they can help the Scrum Team succeed, for example by providing necessary resources of useful feedback to the team.

Solutions: False, True, True, False, True, False

Manager

Question	True	False
The Scrum Master is a management position.		
The Scrum Master manages people.		
The Scrum Master manages the adoption and implementation of Scrum.		
One of the management duties of the Scrum Master is impediment removal.		

This title of this stance is perhaps the most surprising one to people. When learning about Scrum, we early on understand that the Scrum Team as a whole is self-managing and that neither the Product Owner nor the Scrum Master is in charge of the Developers. Then how is the Scrum Master a manager?

In this context, we need to separate the terms "manager" and "management" from the notion of hierarchy and orders, with which they are often used interchangeably. For our purposes, we understand the activity of management as defining a goal and continuously taking the necessary steps towards achieving that goal.

In this sense, the Scrum Master can be described as a manager of the process, not of people. They manage the process of Scrum and its adoption. This entails three key activities:

- Managing the way in which Scrum is understood in the organization. This means having an understanding of the existing level of knowledge and understanding and taking actions to improve this level. Specific actions may include consulting, coaching, training, and teaching across all levels of the organization.

- Managing the way in which Scrum is applied. Especially when first introducing Scrum, it is crucial for the Scrum Master to have a high degree of awareness of how both the organization and the individual Scrum Team are applying Scrum. Subsequently, they will take necessary measures to move the application of Scrum closer to the ideas defined in the Scrum Guide. Specific actions for this, again, include consulting, coaching, training, and teaching across all levels of the organization.
- Removing structural impediments hindering the success of Scrum. Most Scrum Teams will eventually face organizational impediments that make applying Scrum by the book impossible. Here it is the responsibility of the Scrum Master to take all necessary actions to initiate change in the organization towards conditions that are favorable for the proper application of Scrum.

Solutions: True, False, True, True

Mentor

Question	True	False
Mentoring is basically the same as coaching.		
A Scrum Master should mentor not just their team but also stakeholders if possible.		

The Scrum Master acts as a mentor with regard to agility and Scrum. As the Scrum Master is ideally the most knowledgable on the topics within the team and one of the most knowledgable within the organization, they provide mentoring for individuals, teams, and the organization.

Mentoring is distinct from coaching in that coaching does not necessarily require expertise on the specific subject matter. When coaching a Product Owner, for example, the Scrum Master does not necessarily have to know the right answer to the Product Owner's problem, but only help guide them onto the right path. The Product Owner solves their own problem with the help of the Scrum Master.

Mentoring, on the other hand, requires in-depth knowledge, skills, and experience. The mentees benefit from the vast resources that the Scrum Master can provide. A Scrum Master who has experienced a lot of Scrum environments, led multiple Scrum introductions, and possibly even scaled Scrum within organizations will have practical knowledge that can help their current Scrum Team to avoid the mistakes of others.

A powerful application of the Mentor stance is towards stakeholders. When a Scrum Team is lucky enough to have stakeholders who are open to understanding the team's way of work, the Scrum Master helps shape the stakeholders' understanding. They can provide examples of previous successes and failures, prepare the stakeholders for what to expect, and help them gain a better understanding of how best to support the team.

Solutions: False, True

Teacher

Question	True	False
The Scrum Master teaches the team only about Scrum.		
The Teacher stance is only relevant in the early phases of adopting Scrum.		
Depending on the circumstances, a Scrum Master might want to organize formal training sessions.		

The Scrum Guide defines the accountability of the Scrum Master in the following way:

"The Scrum Master is accountable for establishing Scrum as defined in the Scrum Guide. They do this by helping everyone understand Scrum theory and practice, both within the Scrum Team and the organization."[14]

A key stance for the Scrum Master to take towards this is that of the Teacher. Especially when Scrum is initially introduced and in the early phases of its adoption, there is a need for a lot of theoretical input. Those using Scrum and those in their immediate surroundings need to understand a number of important things:

- Why do we take agile approaches at all? Why don't we just stick to a waterfall approach?
- How does Scrum work? What accountabilities, rules, events, artifacts, etc. exist? How do we practically implement those?
- What is "core Scrum" and what are additional, useful practices? Are things like user stories, planning poker, and the "Scrum Board" really part of Scrum? And if not, should we still use them?

- How do teams work together successfully? What role do common goals play in that? How do teams deal with arising impediments?

Even once Scrum has been adopted, the Teacher stance will remain relevant, as due to complexity, new issues will arise that warrant teaching the team, the organization, and the stakeholders new tools, methods, and approaches. In this, the stance of the Teacher needs to be carefully balanced against that of the Coach. While it does make sense to provide theoretical input, some things should be discovered by the team on their own with the guidance of coaching.
The goal of good Scrum Master work is to empower others. The Scrum Master must determine for each case which approach will lead to better long term results: giving the right answers or letting the other person fail and learn from their failure.

The specific teaching format can vary according to what is needed and what is possible. This can include formal training sessions, regular education sessions, and 1-on-1 discussions.

Solutions: False, False, True

Impediment Remover

Question	True	False
One way in which the Scrum Master supports their team is by removing obstacles to their productivity.		
The Scrum Master should themselves remove every impediment they identify.		

The Scrum Master seeks to create an environment, where the Scrum Team can reach peak productivity in value generation. Therefore, a key job of the Scrum Master is to remove obstacles that slow the team down and lower its productivity. These obstacles are what we refer to as "impediments".

There is a large number of possible impediments that can cause problems for the team. Some examples are:
- high technical debt in the product,
- pressure on the Scrum Team from management,
- outdated tools in the development, and
- conflicts arising within the team.

The Scrum Master should aim towards understanding the specific problems and working towards their removal. It is important to understand that this does not necessarily mean that the Scrum Master themselves removes the impediments, but merely that they work towards the removal.

Fixing every problem of a team is the previously discussed misunderstood stance of the Super Hero. Doing so will lead to lower self-management capability and make the Scrum Team become dependent on their Scrum Master. Instead, a Scrum Master should evaluate carefully whether an impediment can reasonably be solved by the Scrum Team.

A newly created team, which has not yet grown into effective self-management, might require the Scrum Master to actively facilitate conflict resolution even for relatively minor conflicts. On the other hand, a mature team that has been working together for years should be capable of resolving upcoming conflicts on its own without the active intervention of the Scrum Master.

The impediments which the Scrum Master addresses themselves are those that exceed the current level of self-management. Especially structural/organizational topics tend to fall into this category. For example, the Developers on the Scrum Team might work in multiple development efforts at the same time, because the management wants to ensure their full utilization. This would lower the Developers' focus and possibly their collaboration. Here it would be the Scrum Master's job to work with management and get them to understand the costs to the team's effectiveness that this brings.

The specific tactics used for impediment removal are very dependent on the individual case and the situation. They do, however, usually require the Scrum Master to have a good understanding of
- the current level of self-management,
- previously solved impediments,
- currently existing impediments, which should be visualized,
- the organization and, to some extend, office politics.

Solutions: True, False

Change Agent

Question	True	False
The Scrum Master is a change agent only within their own team.		
Change towards better environments for Scrum Teams is a linear process.		

The final stance described by Overeem is that of the Change Agent. As we deepen our understanding of Scrum, we realize that in order to implement a truly successful product development effort with Scrum, we need to create the right conditions. Scrum Teams do not exist in a vacuum but are embedded in larger organizations, typically companies.

In order to get the best results, this environment in which the Scrum Team exists must change as well. Two very typical examples from the corporate world where are the following:

1. Scrum Teams need freedom and empowerment for self-management. When dealing with a company in which the classic command-and-control culture is still very much alive, there will inevitably be clashes. Managers with a traditional mindset may demand a final say in the Product Backlog, the right to assign tasks to individual Developers, or weekly formal status reports on the "progress of the project".

2. Scrum Teams are to be understood as teams and their members need to be able to focus on the work of the Scrum Team as much as possible. In many (especially larger) corporations, it is common for people to be assigned to a multitude of projects or assignments. This is often due to a lack of clear priorities and the

notion that maximizing the utilization of people, i.e. keeping them busy as much as possible, leads to the best overall results.

In those cases, and cases like them, the Scrum Master is responsible for working towards changing the status quo of the organization towards one, in which the ideal conditions for a Scrum Team are met.

The specific methods for how to do this are very dependent on the existing conditions. Any transformation begins with awareness of a need for change. The Scrum Master must create transparency on how the current situation is creating impediments to the Scrum Team and thus to the larger organizational goals.
An existing willingness for change needs to be fostered with knowledge and support. The Scrum Master must help those very open to the ideas and especially those who are curious but still skeptical to understand the process of change. The direction of change needs to be clear, the reasons for specific actions must be understandable to all and those that are directly affected must be addressed with genuine empathy.
Change needs to be managed. The Scrum Master must continue to guide the change as it progresses and involve members of the leadership in the process. The goal should be to let the change continue with ever-less active involvement from the Scrum Master.

These steps are not linear, however. Different departments, groups, even individual people will be at different points. There will be back and forth all along the way. The crucial thing for the Scrum Master in his stance of Change Agent is to create transparency over the need for and way of change in a way that those targeted can understand it and feel comfortable with the change.

Solutions: False, False

Changes to the Scrum Team

Question	True	False
Members of the Scrum Team should be changed frequently to add fresh inputs.		
Members of the Scrum Team should never be changed, as this decreases the team's productivity.		
Scrum can only be done with feature teams.		
Changes towards feature teams will lower productivity in the short run.		
Scaling the number of members on a Scrum Team proportionally scales its productivity.		

The Scrum Team is described in the Scrum Guide as a "cohesive unit"[15]. For a Scrum Team to perform well, it is not merely necessary for tools and processes to be in place, but for the individuals within the team to collaborate well. A Scrum Team is more than a group of people working together within a setting that uses Scrum, but rather are an actual team. As such, it is important to understand team dynamics and how they affect changes to the Scrum Team.

In a perfect world, Scrum Team members could be exchanged immediately once it becomes necessary. If for a few Sprints there is no need for the skills for individual developers, they could be removed from the team, possibly replaced by others with a more fitting skill set, and brought back once their skill set is needed again.
In the real world, however, this would likely have serious negative effects and should be done carefully. To understand why let's have a look at one of the most

fundamental models of team dynamics again: the Tuckman Model.

Bruce Tuckman described a model describing how groups of people work together to address problems in four phases:

1. Forming: the group is coming together, learning about the problems, getting to know each other, and beginning the work.
2. Storming: as different people with different personalities, ideas, values, and approaches work together over extended periods of time, disagreements and conflicts will arise.
3. Norming: if the team is able to resolve their disagreements, they create a common set of practices, standards, implicit values, and working agreements.
4. Performing: once the team has found its way of work, they are able to focus on delivering results and performing well at their tasks.

Additionally, it has been suggested that the last two phases tend to happen again and again as the team re-norms with changing challenges.
While this model is very abstract, it holds true surprisingly well in real-world applications and is something a good Scrum Master should be aware of.

Creating changes to the composition of a Scrum Team would lead to a change in the way the team is working. A new forming would take place, as the new members need to get to know the work and the existing members and new members get to know each other. In most cases, a storming phase will take place, which temporarily reduces the productivity of the Scrum Team until a new norming and eventually performing phase kicks in.
Therefore, changes to the composition of a Scrum Team should be done with caution. If changes in the Scrum

Team allow the team to deliver better performance in the long run, they should be done. However, it must be kept in mind that any change will likely reduce the team's performance in the short run.

Teams organize around problems, the forming phase is the one where the team gets to know the (kind of) problems it will be dealing with. If the nature of the problems rapidly changes, similar effects can be seen when staffing changes take place. A very common occurrence of this in Scrum environments is when teams transition from component/layer teams to feature teams.

Component teams, also called layer teams, are teams that specialize in specific components or layers of a product. In software development, this might be specific modules of the product or the entire front-end layer of it. Such splits are common and not incompatible with Scrum. As long as the sum of all Scrum Teams working on a product can deliver integrated increments every Sprint, component teams are a valid approach.

Feature teams, on the other hand, are teams that are capable of delivering features and work across all components or layers of the product. In an environment where only one Scrum Team works on a product, the Scrum Team is by default a feature team, as it is cross-functional. In scaled Scrum environments, multiple feature teams can exist, meaning all Scrum Teams work across all components and layers.

A key benefit of feature teams is the reduction of dependencies during development. Within a feature team, all skills necessary to develop a feature are present. In a component team environment, individual features must be broken down into tasks regarding their different components, those tasks need to be worked on by individual component teams, and finally the result must be integrated. This requires a lot of coordination and communication effort between the team, which may slow down the overall development.

When transitioning from component teams to feature teams, the nature of the work an individual team works on changes dramatically. Whereas the teams only worked on individual layers or components, they now need to work across the entire product. This change will require the team to become accustomed to the new types of problems and adjust itself, i.e. it will need to re-form and will subsequently re-storm and re-norm before coming back to performance again.

Introducing new challenges and new people can have unforeseen consequences. The simple managerial arithmetic of doubling the number of team members to double the performance of the team simply does not work. As we have seen, Scrum Teams - and teams in general - are complex constructs, where the relationship between a specific action and the effect that action has, simply cannot be known for sure in advance. This is a key reason for allowing teams to self-manage; the team knows more about its current status, struggles, and dynamics than any outside manager could. They are closer to the information, have higher transparency, and are thus able to better inspect and adapt.

Solutions: False, False, False, True, False

Scrum Events

Scrum's key purpose is to enable empirical process control to manage risks. While the artifacts, which we will discuss in greater length in a separate chapter, provide the necessary transparency, the Scrum Events serve as opportunities for inspection and adaptation.
All Scrum Events serve a crucial purpose with regards to empirical process control and are therefore mandatory.

The Sprint

The Sprint is described in the Scrum Guide as the "heartbeat of Scrum"[16]. It acts as a container for the other four events, as well as all activities that are done to generate value.

Sprints are what make Scrum iterative. Sprints are of fixed length and no longer than one month. Within that one month or less, the Scrum Team
- decides on its work (Sprint Planning),
- implements Product Backlog items towards the Sprint Goal,
- frequently inspects and adapts its work plan (Daily Scrum),
- inspects the results with key stakeholders and incorporates those changes into the Product Backlog (Sprint Review), and
- looks back on the Sprint and determines process improvements (Sprint Retrospective).

A Sprint can be seen as a small project of
- fixed time: the timebox defined by the Scrum Team, no longer than one month,
- constant or improving quality: at least compliant to the Definition of Done,

- roughly constant cost: the amount of work time and resources invested into a Sprint can usually be forecast relatively well, and
- variable scope: the Scrum Team works towards achieving the Sprint Goal, but might make changes to the scope if necessary.

The Sprint length can be changed, though this should be done with caution. Empirical process control is built on comparing the results of different experiments. Comparing two Sprint of the same length is easier and the results are therefore more reliable than comparing a one-week Sprint with a one-month Sprint. Sprint changes should be handled similarly to staff changed in the Scrum Team: as needed but keeping in mind the short-term downside effects.

Sprint Planning

Question	True	False
The Sprint Planning consists of three phases.		
The Developers craft the Sprint Goal.		
The Sprint Goal may not be changed during a Sprint, even as more is learned.		
The Developers pull items from the Product Backlog based on their Definition of Ready.		
If there is a lack in clarity of Product Backlog items, the Sprint Planning's timebox may be extended until all things are cleared up.		
The Sprint Backlog is not finalised at the end of the Sprint Planning and may change throughout the Sprint.		

The purpose of the work of the Scrum Team each Sprint is to create value by building potentially releasable, Done increments. In order to start this process, the Scrum Team needs to get an understanding of three key parameters laid out in the Scrum Guide:

1. How can the Sprint be used to create something of value? What is the general direction in which the team wants to head with its work?
2. What is actually achievable within the Sprint? What Product Backlog items can actually be implemented with the given time and resources?
3. How can the chosen work be done? What initial plan can be devised to implement the selected items?

The parameters should not be understood as sequential steps or phases. Rather, they affect each other throughout the Sprint Planning, and going back and forth may be necessary. To illustrate, let's look at an example:

The Product Owner proposes in the beginning, how the Sprint may help the product gain value. This sets the direction for the Sprint, which should also be reflected in the Product Backlog. The Scrum Team may use this to draft an initial Sprint Goal.
The Scrum Team now looks at the Product Backlog and the Developers pull as many items from it as they believe can be achieved. Here, it may be realized that with the given resources, the Developers will not be able to implement enough items to achieve the Sprint Goal. This may lead to a re-negotiation of the Sprint Goal draft and possibly a change in the items selected for the Sprint.
Once the preliminary selection of Product Backlog items for the Sprint is done, the Developers begin to devise a plan on how to implement these items. This often includes decomposing items into smaller work units. In this process, previously undiscovered dependencies may be revealed. It may also be learned that the initial estimations of the effort required were likely incorrect and need to be updated.
This in turn may lead to the Developers changing their minds on what items can be implemented. Potentially, this affects the preliminary Sprint Goal, which may need to be changed.

While not every Sprint Planning happens in the way described above, it can happen. Therefore, the Scrum Guide does not outline three steps of three phases of a Sprint Planning, but merely points out that those three topics need to be addressed and requires a Sprint Goal to be done before the end of the Sprint Planning.

To understand the Sprint Planning better, let's look at the key elements and actions relevant during a Sprint Planning:
- the value proposition,
- the Sprint Goal,
- the selection of Product Backlog items, and
- the implementation planning.

Solutions: False, False, True, False, False, True

The Value Proposition

While "value proposition" is not a formal term used in the Scrum Guide, it describes the activity of the Product Owner quite well. The Product Owner has a vision for their product, which is broken down into Product Goals, which we will look at in greater detail when discussing the Product Backlog. Product Goals usually require multiple Sprints to be achieved, thus they are broken down into smaller steps: the work of single Sprints.

The Product Owner proposes how the Sprint can help the product gain value by working toward the current Product Goal. This proposition typically forms the basis for the Sprint Goal. Good Product Owners have always made it clear to their Scrum Teams what the value proposition for the Sprint is. With the 2020 update to the Scrum Guide, this topic was introduced as mandatory to underline the importance of this proposition in forming a common goal for the Sprint.

The Sprint Goal

The Sprint Goal is crafted by the entire Scrum Team and committed to by the Developers. It defines the purpose of the Sprint. The Scrum Guide describes each Sprint to be comparable to a short project. In that sense, the Sprint Goal is the project goal of our maximum one-month-long project.

The Sprint Goal is fixed and does not change. Rather, the work necessary to achieve it may need to change as more is learned. A well-formulated Sprint Goal allows the Developers to simultaneously have a clear direction for their work and at the same time flexibility to adjust their work if necessary.

The Selection of Product Backlog Items

The Developers and Product Owner discuss what items would serve the Sprint Goal. Subsequently, the Developers pull those items from the Product Backlog that are deemed most useful to achieve the Sprint Goal. These usually are all high-ranked items in the Product Backlog, though this is not always necessarily the case.

The decision of how many items will be pulled is up to the Developers. While the Product Owner may encourage the Developers to pull more and work with them to negotiate the scope of individual Product Backlog items, the final decision is left to the Developers.

Selecting Product Backlog items for the Sprint is made significantly easier if the Product Backlog is in a well-refined state. However, in a complex environment, this can not always be ensured. For example, the recent Sprint Review may have revealed new critical information that necessitates a drastic change in priorities, leading to items rising in the Product Backlog and becoming crucial that were not previously refined.

Such cases are the reason for the lack of a mandatory Definition of Ready in Scrum. Many Scrum Teams create internal conventions on what should be ensured before a Product Backlog item is deemed ready to be pulled from the Product Backlog. Such internal agreements are a useful tool to create transparency between the individual Developers as well as between the Developers and the Product Owner.

However, in the scenario described above, such a "Definition of Ready" might lead to the team not being able to plan their Sprint, as no "Ready" items are available to be pulled.

Choosing to form a Sprint Goal based only on the "Ready" items would violate the idea that the Scrum Team always works on what is believed to create the greatest value at the time. In such a case, the Scrum

Team would instead try to use the available time to get a better understanding of the items and make a plan on whatever information is known at the time. The timebox must still be maintained and if necessary, the Developers leave the Sprint Planning without a truly clear and well-decomposed Sprint Backlog.

In Scrum, the Sprint Backlog - unlike the Sprint Goal - is dynamic in nature. As more is learned, for example through analysis and implementation, it can and should be updated. In the given scenario, the Developers create an initial Sprint Backlog that serves the Sprint Goal and are fully conscious that there may be potentially dramatic changes to the Sprint Backlog throughout the Sprint. Such a situation is not desirable and fortunately does not happen regularly. If, however, it does take place, a good idea is to later evaluate the reasons that lead up to it in the Sprint Retrospective.

The Implementation Planning

The Developers plan how the work selected can be achieved. How this is done depends on the context of the development. Developers may choose to simply discuss the items, create designs, look at source code together and even consult outside experts. Ultimately, it is up to the Developers as a whole to create a plan on how to implement the selected items and get them into a Done state.

Depending on how likely things are to change throughout the Sprint, it may make sense to plan the entire work or to merely plan for a few days and inspect and adapt along the way, making use of the Daily Scrum to coordinate further "mini-plannings" during the Sprint.

Often, work is decomposed into work units of one day or less, as this allows the team to inspect the progress towards the Sprint Goal during their Daily Scrums and make subsequent adaptations. This is, however, optional and left up to the Developers.

Daily Scrum

Question	True	False
The Daily Scrum must be held at the same time and in the same place every day.		
The Daily Scrum is used to inspect progress towards the Sprint Goal and adapt the Sprint Backlog.		
The Developers can use the Daily Scrum to identify impediments that might either be resolved by them or handed to the Scrum Master.		
Daily Scrums helps the Developers connect, which is particularly important when they are not working together in the same place.		
The entire Scrum Team attends and participates in the Daily Scrum.		
An important output of the Daily Scrum can be a status report to management.		
The Scrum Master does not participate in the Daily Scrum, they only ensure that it takes place and that it is kept within the 15 minute timebox.		
Lowering the frequency of the Daily Scrum increases risks, slows down impediment resolution and may lead to growing disconnect between Developers.		

Following the Sprint Planning, the work on implementing the selected Product Backlog items begins. The Sprint Backlog outlines the plan for implementing the items in order to achieve the Sprint Goal. As previously discussed, in complex environments, plans may need to be altered once new information becomes available and situations change.

In Scrum, not only do we use empirical process control on the large scale by inspecting and adapting from Sprint to Sprint, but also within Sprint. The plan devised in the Sprint Planning, i.e. the Sprint Backlog, needs to be frequently inspected and adapted as well. This is the key purpose of the Daily Scrum.

As with all Scrum Events, each Daily Scrum is ideally held at the same time and in the same place. This makes coordination simpler and reduces complexity. It is much simpler for a team to hold every Daily Scrum at 9am than to have a different time each day of the week or even to change the times from week to week.
This is not to say that if half of the Developers cannot attend at 9am on one specific day but could attend and 9:30am, the Daily Scrum should not be moved. The consistency of time and place is a tool for reducing complexity, not a dogma.

Until its 2017 edition, the Scrum Guide defined the format of the Daily Scrum. Each Developer had to explain:
- what they did yesterday towards achieving the Sprint Goal,
- what they plan to do today towards achieving the Sprint Goal, and
- if they identified impediments to themselves or the Developers.[17]

This format, colloquially referred to as "the three questions", is still frequently used to this day. The 2017 Scrum Guide, however, only listed it as an exemplary format[18] and the 2020 Scrum Guide removed it entirely.

The format is now left to the Developers. Some may choose to continue the three questions format, others may discuss the state of the Sprint Backlog by using a Kanban-Board-like visualization, yet others may choose yet another way. The focus of the meeting should be on the progress towards the Sprint Goal and on creating an actionable plan for the next day of work. Beyond this, the Daily Scrum provides a number of further benefits to the Developers:
- It provides a platform for quick decision-making.
- It offers an opportunity to identify impediments. These can either be resolved on the spot, it can be decided to resolve them at a later point in time, or it can be decided that it is an impediment that should be handed over to the Scrum Master.
- It defines at least 15 minutes per day during which the entire group of Developers come together. This is particularly important with teams that are not co-located, i.e. that do not share a physical office space.

A common misconception of the Daily Scrum is the idea that the entire Scrum Team is supposed to attend. Rather, the Daily Scrum is a meeting of, for, and by the Developers. The Scrum Master and Product Owner should only attend if they also work as Developers. Stakeholders or members of the management should also not attend.

The reason for this is two-fold. For one, changing the attendance of the event changes the nature of the meeting. Having a Product Owner or even manager present will likely change the nature of the Daily Scrum from the open and transparent inspect-and-adapt meeting is meant to be towards a status update. The Daily Scrum is not a status meeting and its output is an adapted Sprint Backlog, not a status report to anybody.
Secondly, the Developers are self-managing and as such must self-manage their meeting. Whether or not Developers manage to conduct effective Daily Scrums

and maintain the timebox is a valuable indicator of the self-management maturity level of the Developers.

The role of the Scrum Master regarding the Daily Scrum is limited. While in many companies the Scrum Master "facilitates" or rather moderates the Daily Scrum, this undermines the self-management of the Developers. The Scrum Master's responsibility is only to teach the Developers to keep the Daily Scrum within the 15-minute timebox and to ensure that the Daily Scrum takes place every day.

A frequent point of discussion between Developers and Scrum Masters concerns the necessity of the Daily Scrum in general or its frequency. For Developers to support the idea of a daily 15-minute meeting, it is beneficial for them to understand the purpose of it. Therefore, it is important for a Scrum Master to ensure the Developers understand not just the mechanics of the Daily Scrum, but its purpose within Scrum and the risks that would be created if it were dropped entirely or held less frequently. These include the points addressed above:
- Opportunities to inspect and adapt are lost, which increases risk as the Developers continue working according to a plan that is not the most up-to-date.
- Impediments are raised later, which means they will likely be resolved later.
- The team will lose the chance to coordinate all together on a daily basis, which may lead to a growing disconnect between them.

Coaching Developers towards understanding the value and importance of Daily Scrums is one of the key services a Scrum Master can provide to the Developers.

Solutions: False, True, True, True, False, False, True, True

Sprint Review

Question	True	False
The purpose of the Sprint Review is inspecting the Increment and adapting the Product Backlog.		
Developers may show individual features on their local, not yet integrated code basis.		
All work conducted during the Sprint is inspected during the Sprint Review.		
The Product Owner is responsible for ensuring the transparency of the Increment.		
When there is a lack of openness during the Sprint Review, stakeholders may eventually get upset and frustrate.		

Every Sprint is a small experiment: during the Sprint Planning, the Scrum Team creates a hypothesis for what would be the best way to deliver value. After implementing Product Backlog items towards the Sprint Goal, it must now be verified whether that original hypothesis was valid. This is done during the Sprint Review, which is intended to be the key opportunity for the Scrum Team and the stakeholders to inspect the result of the Sprint (i.e. the latest Increment).

The feedback and discussions during the Sprint Review are key inputs for the Product Owner. A good Sprint Review serves to better clarify the needs and wishes of the stakeholder based upon the current situation of the product, which subsequently may lead to an adaptation of the Product Backlog. Thus, the Sprint Review serves as an indirect input for the upcoming Sprint Planning.

For a Sprint Review to be successful in serving empirical process control, two important parameters must be assured: the Increment must be transparent and those doing the inspection must be open with each other.

The most crucial point for the transparency of the Increment is whether it is Done according to the Definition of Done. The participants of the Sprint Review inspect an Increment that could be released into the market. Typical anti-patterns for this are:
- inspecting "Increments" that are not yet fully tested
- inspecting "Increments" that are not yet fully documented
- inspecting "Increments" that are not yet integrated, e.g. every Developer shows individual features on their own version of the code, rather than on the fully integrated code basis.

When one or more of these points apply, the inspection and subsequently the adaptation is flawed. For example, the stakeholders may believe that the product could be released immediately, even though further testing is necessary which might reveal errors that take weeks to fix. Or the Product Owner may believe that since the Developers "finished" 12 items, they will likely finish 12 items in each other coming Sprint, even though the Developers would have only managed to get 8 items Done. On this basis, the Product Owner makes release forecasts to stakeholders that are inherently flawed.
Therefore, it is crucial to follow the Definition of Done and to not present Increments that include anything not yet fully Done.

The stakeholders and Scrum Team conduct a common inspection. Thus, artifact transparency is necessary. As the "manager of the Scrum process", it is the responsibility of the Scrum Master to ensure a high level of artifact transparency. Furthermore, the openness of Scrum Team members and stakeholders towards one another is necessary.

Even if an Increment is transparent in the sense that it complies with a Definition of Done that is visible to and understood by everyone, the inspection can still go wrong if those doing the inspection are not open with each other. This is particularly true for a lack of openness by the stakeholders.

The stakeholders participate in the Sprint Review so that they can provide immediate feedback, which subsequently affects the next steps. If this feedback is not provided at all or if it is not provided openly, key information might be missed. A common pattern is stakeholders who are afraid of open criticism.

Imagine a product development with Scrum with an external customer, i.e. the development takes place in another organization than that of the customer. The Scrum Team invites the stakeholders, typically into their office. Now the customer is in an environment that is not their own, with people whom they don't know very well, often with more members of the Scrum Team present than stakeholders. When observing things that are not to their liking, many stakeholders will decide to keep feedback short, especially critical feedback. This arises out of a cultural understanding that criticizing the product is equal to criticizing those that built the product.

In Scrum, we need to break with such patterns to allow for proper inspection. Here it is one of the responsibilities of a Scrum Master to work with the stakeholder to get them to the understanding, that openness is necessary for mutually beneficial product development. The alternative is usually either permanently dissatisfied stakeholders or even stakeholders that emotionally explode at some point.

Solutions: True, False, False, False, True

Sprint Retrospective

The Sprint Retrospective is the last of the Scrum Events to take place within a Sprint. At this point in the Sprint, the work of the Sprint has been planned, executed with repeated inspection and adaptation of the plan, and the result has been inspected with key stakeholders. Two things are likely to be true at this point:

1. Not everything went perfectly during the Sprint.
2. The situation in the next Sprint will likely not be identical to the one in the current Sprint.

Therefore, we need to inspect all aspects of our way of working and, while doing that, keep in mind likely changes that will come up in the near future. Based on these inspections, we need to make relevant adaptations to our way of working.

To provide a platform for this inspection and adaptation, Scrum mandates the Sprint Retrospective. The entire Scrum Team gathers, evaluates their situation, and creates plans for improving further.

Scrum does not dictate any specific format for the Sprint Retrospective. Some teams may choose to hold an open discussion, others may utilize metrics gathered throughout the Sprint, yet others may run Sprint Retrospectives facilitated by the Scrum Master using a 5-phase-model.

Arguably more crucial than the format is the openness of the Scrum Team members towards one another. Inspection can only occur properly if transparency exists, metaphorically speaking: if all cards are on the table. This requires those participating in the Sprint Retrospective to be honest and to voice their concerns and ideas proactively.

The Sprit Retrospective is not the only opportunity for inspecting and adapting processes, but it is certainly the one with the most potential impact. Ensuring that this potential is realized is the responsibility of the Scrum Master, who must ensure that everybody understands the purpose of the Sprint Retrospective, feels comfortable sharing their thoughts, and addresses their concerns towards the other Scrum Team members.

It is important to keep in mind the nature of empiricism when identifying possible process improvements during the Sprint Retrospective. Anything defined in the Sprint Retrospective as an action item is a hypothesis, not a certainty. We cannot know for sure whether making a specific change to our way of work will lead to better results; it could not have any relevant effect, no effect at all, or possibly even an adverse effect. The next Sprint is used as an experiment with regard to this hypothesis. The Scrum Team applies the change and evaluates - e.g. in their next Sprint Retrospective - what effect it had and whether it should remain to be changed again.

In such experimental loops of hypothesis creation and hypothesis verification or falsification, the Scrum Team adjusts its way of work towards greater effectiveness and efficiency in light of ever-changing conditions.

Artifacts

For empirical process control to work effectively, it must be ensured that all those involved in the inspection and adaptation have the same information available, so that decisions are made on the same basis. This is what we refer to as transparency and the three artifacts and their respective commitments are Scrum's key tool for creating this transparency.

In the 2017 edition of the Scrum Guide, the Definition of Done - which is now considered a commitment on the Increment - was in fact listed as an explicit example of transparency:

"Significant aspects of the process must be visible to those responsible for the outcome. Transparency requires those aspects to be defined by a common standard so observers share a common understanding of what is being seen.
For example
- A common language referring to the process must be shared by all participants; and,
- Those performing the work and those inspecting the resulting increment must share a common definition of 'Done'."[19]

To illustrate the need for such transparency, let's imagine a hypothetical scenario without a Definition of Done:

Key stakeholders call a Product Owner and ask if an important feature is already done. The Product Owner consults with the Developers, who tell them that it is done. The Product Owner carries this information back to the stakeholders. The stakeholders are delighted and request to have the feature available on their systems as soon as possible. The entire process of getting the feature to the stakeholders ends up taking three weeks and the stakeholders are extremely unsatisfied with this.

While the stakeholders understood "done" as being able to have it available with the click of a button. The Product Owner understood "done" as having the feature developed but not yet put into a releasable state. The Developers understood "done" as having the business logic behind the feature implemented, but not having done any significant testing done yet.

In this example, none of the groups involved is incorrect. Everybody merely had a different understanding of what "done" means. To avoid the resulting confusion and miscommunication, a common standard should be defined what constitutes "done". This is the basis for the Definition of Done.

Each artifact and its corresponding commitment serves the purpose of making important information available and commonly understandable. The goal is to allow for better inspection and better subsequent adaptation.

Product Backlog

The 2020 Scrum Guide defines the Product Backlog as follow:

"The Product Backlog is an emergent, ordered list of what is needed to improve the product. It is the single source of work undertaken by the Scrum Team."

All work that might be done by the Scrum Team is listed in the Product Backlog, even if not all of it will eventually be implemented. The Product Backlog represents the Product Owner's current understanding of what will help the product increase in value. As this estimation will change, new ideas will arise and others may be discarded. This is why we speak of an "emergent ... list"[20] or, as the 2017 Scrum Guide put it, a "living artifact"[21].

Those items that are deemed currently more helpful in generating value are ordered to be further at the top, those deemed less helpful further to the bottom. This assessment will change over time as well, thus the order of the Product Backlog will change.

The Product Backlog that is made available to those involved in the product development effort creates transparency about:
- all the steps that are currently considered as adding value to the product, and
- the Product Owner's current assessment of the priorities.

These two factors are crucial information for Scrum Team and stakeholders.
When, for example, a stakeholder wishes to know what the likely next steps for the product development are, they only need to have a look at the Product Backlog's top items, as these are the ones likely to be implemented in the coming Sprints.

When, for example, a Developer comes up with an idea and wants to check if it has already been considered, they can look at the Product Backlog and check if it is already included.

Furthermore, the Product Backlog is used by the Scrum Team to get items from an idea in the mind of a stakeholder or the Product Owner towards something that can be implemented by the Developers. Additional descriptions, estimates, and other details may be added during refinement activities and items may be broken down into smaller packages that can each be implemented in one Sprint. In this sense, the Product Backlog serves to create a common understanding (i.e. transparency) within the Scrum Team about the requirements of upcoming work.

The Product Backlog shows the direction of the product development. This is further strengthened by the Product Goal, the Product Backlog's commitment. The Product Goal describes a desired future state of the product. The work of the Scrum Team is focused on achieving the current Product Goal by implementing Product Backlog items. Those items are arranged by the Product Owner to work towards delivering value by achieving the Product Goal.

A Product Goal thus creates an overarching direction for the Scrum Team and makes the current direction of the product development explicitly clear to everyone involved. Every stakeholder can understand the goal that is currently pursued by looking at the Product Goal and the specific steps towards this by looking at the individual items at the top of the Product Backlog.

It is important to note that the Product Goal is replaced over time. A Product Goal is either achieved by the Scrum Team or is abandoned. In either case, it is replaced with a new one. There is always a Product Goal defining the overarching direction.

Sprint Backlog

While the Product Backlog creates transparency about the plans for the product, the Sprint Backlog creates transparency about the plans for the Sprint. The Sprint Backlog is an internal artifact of the Developers and serves to make three core aspects transparent:

- the reason for the work of the Sprint, i.e. the Sprint Goal
- the specific items that should be implemented to achieve the Sprint Goal, i.e. the selected Product Backlog items
- the plan on how to implement the Product Backlog items

The Scrum Guide describes the Sprint Backlog as a "highly visible, real-time picture of the work that the Developers plan to accomplish during the Sprint".[22]
There is no prescribed method, tool, or technique for how a Sprint Backlog should look like. Some teams may choose to write up their plans and progress in shared text documents, others may use Kanban-inspired boards that track the progress. The important thing is that the way in which the Sprint Backlog is made available serves to maximize the Developers' ability to understand the current status of the work and the further plans.

The Sprint Backlog is inspected and adapted as frequently as necessary, but at least once per day during the Daily Scrum.

The Sprint Goal, the Sprint Backlog's commitment, makes the reason for the work of the Sprint transparent to all Developers. It serves as a guideline for the decisions of the Developers as individuals and as a group throughout the Sprint. Especially when the Developers learn during the Sprint that not all selected

Product Backlog items can be achieved, the Sprint Goal is used to define which items are more crucial and which ones are less so.

In such cases, the scope of the Sprint Backlog may need to be reduced. This is done by the Developers and the Product Owner. The Sprint Goal must remain intact, however. If the Sprint Goal becomes obsolete, either because it cannot be achieved anymore or because outside conditions like market situations change, the Sprint is canceled by the Product Owner.

It is important to understand that the Sprint Backlog is not required to serve as a tool to create transparency toward the Product Owner or outsiders. The Developers are self-managing with regard to their work, including the management of their Sprint Backlog. It is their artifact and set up to facilitate their collaboration towards the Sprint Goal. If others can use it to derive useful information, that can be an additional benefit, though the style of the Sprint Backlog should not be changed to accommodate others.

Increment

Question	True	False
During a Sprint, exactly one Increment is produced.		
The Definition of Done is only relevant during the work of the Developers during the Sprint.		
The Definition of Done may contain non-functional requirements such as stability and performance.		
Items that are almost Done may be included in the Increment if the Product Owner agrees to it.		

The Increment is arguably the central artifact of Scrum as it represents the (Done) work of the Scrum Team toward the Product Goal. It creates transparency about the current state of the product development. An Increment must be created at least by the end of each Sprint to allow for inspection during the Sprint Review.

The 2020 Scrum Guide update slightly altered the meaning of "Increment" to include any sum of a previous increment and some amount of new value. Under the 2020 Scrum Guide, a new Increment is thus created when some value is added to a previous increment and ensured to be in compliance with the Definition of Done.[23] Therefore, there may be a number of Increments created during a Sprint, any of which may be released to the product's users at the discretion of the Product Owner.

The Increment's commitment is the Definition of Done, which in older literature may be written as *definition of "done"* based on the pre-2020 Scrum Guide editions. As described in the intro to this chapter, the Definition of Done serves to create a common understanding of what is meant when the Scrum Team considers something to be completed, i.e. "Done". Thereby, the Definition of Done serves a variety of purposes:

- During the Sprint Planning, the Developers create a forecast of how much work they believe they can achieve during the Sprint. If the Developers among themselves have differing understandings of what constitutes a finished Product Backlog item, their opinions of what can be achieved will likely vary widely. If the Product Owner has a higher expectation, they will likely be disappointed by the results of the Sprint, which to them will not be truly completed.

- Throughout the Sprint, it is important for the Developers to have a shared understanding of what work needs to be done to get a Product Backlog item Done, as this will have a direct effect on understanding the progress toward the Sprint Goal and therefore the inspection and adaptation of the Sprint Backlog.

- The Definition of Done typically covers necessary aspects of non-functional requirements, i.e. requirements that are not describing specific (business) functions but rather things like security and performance. These may need to be continuously addressed by the Scrum Team and can therefore be made transparent by adding them to the Definition of Done.

- It ensures that only those Product Backlog items are included in the Increment that are actually completed. Those that are not fully Done, even if they are "99% finished" are not to be included. During the Sprint Review, the Increment is inspected by the Scrum Team and key stakeholders. If un-Done items are included, it becomes harder to assess the true state of the Increment, which makes all subsequent adaptations more difficult.

For example, an item may be included that is almost Done but only lacks a few final tests. During the Sprint Review, the Increment is inspected, and based on that the next steps are planned. During the first days of the next Sprint, the tests are run and reveal significant problems with the item that will require a lot of work to fix. The options would then be to a) spend additional time on fixing the issues, which takes time away from other items that were forecast to be finished in the Sprint, or b) remove the item from the Increment, even though the stockholders have already seen it and might be expecting to receive it in the next release.
Either scenario increases risk, which is exactly what we are trying to mitigate by using Scrum!

The Definition of Done is owned by the Scrum Team. Often, the organization within which the development takes place, e.g. a company, will define minimum quality criteria. In that case, these criteria serve as a minimum Definition of Done, which the Scrum Team may expand upon. The Definition of Done is one subject to inspection and possible adaptation during the Sprint Retrospective.

Solutions: False, False, True, False

Scrum Values

Question	True	False
The Scrum Values are courage, focus, respect, transparency and commitment.		
The Scrum Values have to be agreed upon before starting a development effort with Scrum.		
Living the Scrum Values leads to trust growing within the Scrum Team and between Scrum Team and stakeholders.		

The Scrum Values have been introduced with the 2016 edition of the Scrum Guide. Since then, they are defined to be commitment, courage, focus, openness, and respect.

In the Scrum context, a value can be described as an overarching pattern of behavior, as things that are important to the individuals in the team and that drive them to do certain things and avoid others. A common misconception is that these values need to be studied or otherwise internalized before starting a development effort using Scrum, which is not practically possible. Rather, these values are to be explored empirically during development. The Scrum Guide states: "The Scrum Team members learn and explore the values as they work with the Scrum events and artifacts."[24]

Living these values will lead to better outcomes for the Scrum Team. As the members work together, they should experiment with living these values a bit more, which is likely to produce better results. This serves as a positive feedback loop, which encourages that value further. As time progresses, Scrum Teams should become more proficient with the values. Regularly reflecting on the positive effects of living the values, creating the necessary conditions, and encouraging actions that manifest the values is one of the responsibilities of a Scrum Master.

Let's take a look at the value of focus in a hypothetical scenario. The idea of focus in Scrum is that those in the Scrum Team focus primarily on the work of the Sprint. In many cases, especially in environments new to Scrum, people are involved in multiple projects at the same time and have other responsibilities besides the Scrum Team's work.

The Scrum Team's Scrum Master encourages everybody to try and spend two Sprints focussing primarily on the work of the Scrum Team. All members agree to give it a try as an experiment and not only spend 3.5 hours per day on it but 7 hours. As they now spend twice the time, they should generate twice the results. However, as they focus on the work, they have fewer disturbances through context switches and have more time in which everybody works for the Scrum Team, allowing quicker coordination and better collaboration between them.
They will most likely produce results much better than twice what they were doing before.
The greater value produced will be inspected during the Sprint Review and likely lead to positive feedback from the stakeholders. During the Sprint Retrospective, the Scrum Master encourages everybody to reflect on the outcome of their experiment and to draw meaningful conclusions from it. The Scrum Team just learned the value of focus and its effect on the outcomes generated.

Strongly living the Scrum Values generally leads to better collaboration within the team, as the members are committed to the same goal, focused on the same work, courageous enough to be open about their problems, and respectful towards one another. This is a key contributor to the happiness of the team members, which in turn has a positive effect on productivity.

Furthermore, it generally leads to better interactions with the stakeholders. While especially openness with stakeholders can be difficult in the beginning, once a basis of trust has been established, it becomes much easier to understand the stakeholders and develop the product that the stakeholders will like.

Continuously improving the levels of living the values will grow trust within the Scrum Team and between the Scrum Team and its stakeholders.

Solutions: False, False, True

Scaling Scrum

Question	True	False
In scaled Scrum, the entire Scrum Guide still applies.		
When there are four Scrum Teams working on one product, there should be four Product Owners, one for each Scrum Team.		
A Developer can be a member of multiple Scrum Teams working on the same product.		
Good Product Backlog refinement can make it unnecessary for a Developer to work in multiple Scrum Teams.		
Multiple Scrum Teams working on the same product must have the same Sprint length and starting dates for their Sprints.		
In a scaled Sprint Planning, each team pulls the same number of items into their individual Sprint Backlogs.		
When scaling Scrum, the velocity of individual Scrum Teams is likely to drop.		
Velocity is a useful metric to compare the performance between different Scrum Teams.		
During the Sprint Review, the Increment that is presented is the sum of the work of all the Scrum Teams together.		

The Scrum Guide describes a setup with one Scrum Team, consisting of one Product Owner, one Scrum

Master, and a number of Developers. The team size is stated as "typically 10 or fewer".[25] A team of around 10 people can only work a limited number of hours and only deliver a limited amount of value. If the demand for more value generation exceeds a single Scrum Team's capacities, it can be useful to set up one or more additional Scrum Teams. When multiple Scrum Teams work on the same product, we speak of "scaled Scrum".

While scaling can bring additional complications, it is important to remember that the Scrum Guide in its entirety still applies. Scaling Scrum means taking Scrum and scaling its ideas, rules, and concepts into an environment with more people.
A commonly seen violation of this is product development with multiple Product Owners for one product. When, for example, four Scrum Teams work on the same product, many organizations will assign a separate Product Owner to each team, possibly each with their own Product Backlog, and usually with someone taking on the role of "Lead PO", "Head PO", or "Chief PO".

The motivation for this is understandable: every team has a Product Owner, each of which can focus on their Scrum Team and possibly a smaller part of the product. The issue of who has the final decision is resolved by adding in a level of hierarchy.
This does, however, create problems that are not compatible with Scrum. The Product Owner role is set up to be a part of the team and to be directly accessible by the Developers. Adding a proxy in-between the person inquiring and the person ultimately responsible for giving a proper response delays communication and introduces unnecessary risks. Furthermore, in such a setup, the "Lead PO" would be responsible for maximizing the value delivered by the Scrum Teams, meaning all relevant decisions such as renegotiating the scope of the Sprint Backlog during a Sprint, would need to go to the "Lead PO" anyway.

Scaled Scrum maintains the idea laid out in the chapter on the Product Owner: one Product - one Product Owner - one Product Backlog. This is due to Scrum's inherent link between product, Product Owner, and Product Backlog. The consequence of this can be that the Product Owner may delegate some of the practical work of Product Backlog management to others, while still being accountable for the outcomes.

Unlike the Product Owner, however, there can be multiple Scrum Masters in a scaled Scrum environment. There is no rule on how many teams a Scrum Master should be a part of, but in practice it usually turns out to be two when working a full-time job.

There can obviously be multiple Developers and there is no explicit rule against a Developer being a part of multiple Scrum Teams working on the same product. This may be necessary at times, for example when one person is the only one with specific skills relevant to multiple teams. It should be noted, however, that this dependency of multiple teams on one person can create problems for the teams and that this person will likely lose productivity due to a lack of focus on one Sprint Backlog. Therefore, such set-ups should only be temporary and the Scrum Teams should work towards gaining greater cross-functionality to avoid this in the future.

Scaling Scrum has direct impacts on the creation and refinement of the Product Backlog, the Scrum Events, and the work during the Sprint. Let's have a look at them:

Product Backlog Refinement

Multiple Scrum Teams pulling work from the same Product Backlog means that at any time, more work will have been pulled into Sprint Backlogs and possibly started than with only one team. Therefore, it is a critical goal of Product Backlog refinements to work towards minimizing dependencies between items.
Imagine working with three Scrum Teams, each pulling work into their respective Sprint Backlogs, but crucial items of two teams depend on the third team finishing one of their items. This would lead to an increased risk of Scrum Teams delaying each other and being forced to work on things that are not those items that would generate the highest possible value at the time.

Proper Product Backlog refinement in a scaled Scrum environment tries to make items as independent from each other as possible and, where that is not possible, creates a Product Backlog that is set up to minimize the impact of unavoidable dependencies. By doing this, good Product Backlog management can often make it unnecessary for one Developer to be a member of multiple Scrum Teams.

Sprint

When working with Scrum with multiple teams, it is not necessary for the Sprints of the teams to start at the same time, end at the same time, or even be of the same length. Additional scaling frameworks, such as Nexus, LeSS, or Scrum@Scale, may define additional requirements on this issue, such as common durations or common starting points and Sprint lengths with a common denominator.

The reason many scaling frameworks choose common Sprint lengths and starts is because it synchronizes the (scaled) Scrum Events. For simplicity, the remaining Scrum Events will be described under the assumption of synchronicity.

Sprint Planning

As in one-team-Scrum, the Product Owner presents a value case. Developers from the different Scrum Teams then work with each other and the Product Owner to identify, which Scrum Team should best work on which items in the Sprint. Once the teams have pulled items into their Sprint Backlogs, each team proceeds with regular Sprint Planning activities. During these, further changes to the item selection may become necessary, which are to be resolved by the different Developers in agreement with each other and the Product Owner.

There are no prescribed criteria on how the selection of times into Sprint Backlogs takes place. The number of items or - if used - the sum of Story Points does not need to be equal. Rather, each team should make their forecast of how much they believe to be able to deliver transparent, and the entirety of the Sprint Planning participants should come to an agreement or what would be the best way to generate as much value as possible.

Daily Scrum and Work during the Sprint

Throughout the Sprint, each Scrum Team's Developers conduct their respective Daily Scrum. A possible new output can be that coordination with others Scrum Teams may be necessary for the coming days. Some scaling frameworks prescribe the use of an overarching daily coordination meeting of representatives of the Scrum Teams, mirroring the idea of a Daily Scrum between multiple teams.

The work during the Sprint should take place within the Scrum Teams as much as possible. The extent to which this is possible is a result of the quality of the Product Backlog refinement described earlier. However, there will typically be some coordination effort between the teams required. This is one of the reasons, why the amount of work finished by a Scrum Team in a Sprint, which is often called "velocity", will decrease somewhat in a scaled Scrum environment.

Velocity may often be falsely used by members of management to compare Scrum Teams with each other and possibly even tie rewards such as financial bonuses to it. This is a potentially dangerous action to take as it can create wrong incentives for the teams for two reasons:
- The overarching goal of all of the Scrum Team is to deliver the highest possible value. While velocity can be a useful internal metric for forecasting during Sprint Plannings, it has no direct correlation with value. A Scrum Team that finishes one highly valuable item may have a lower velocity than another one that finishes seven items that generate lower value. The incentive the managers would create is to choose quantity of items over value.

- It places the Scrum Teams, which should share a common goal, into competition with each other. This makes it less likely that the teams will support each other, as support often means sacrificing your own short-term productivity to help someone increase their productivity.

Imagine a scenario where four Scrum Teams have a common problem. After initial assessments, it is determined that this problem will take a lot of time to fix but is highly important. One of the teams is best qualified to take on this problem, so they should volunteer for the common good. If this, however, has negative repercussions on their velocity and therefore on their yearly bonus, they will think twice about volunteering.

The incentive the managers would create is to choose self-interest over common goals.

This coordination between the teams is the responsibility of the teams, specifically of the Developers of each Scrum Team. While in classic project management, there may be coordination between the managers or tech leads of each team, Scrum does not recognize these roles and instead values direct communication. All Scrum Teams are collectively responsible for delivering a common, integrated Increment by the end of the Sprint. Ensuring that the Developers understand this responsibility and offering support for them gaining the necessary competencies is one of the responsibilities of a Scrum Master in a scaled Scrum environment.

All Scrum Teams must adhere to the Definition of Done. Individual teams may define higher standards for themselves, but no team may deliver something that does not completely comply with the product's Definition of Done.

Sprint Review

The Sprint Review has the purpose of inspecting the Increment and adapting the Product Backlog based on the feedback from the attending key stakeholders. This holds true in a scaled Scrum environment, which is why the inspection during the Sprint Review is of one integrated Increment.

Individual Scrum Teams may still present the newly added value that their team created specifically, but this must happen using one integrated, potentially releasable Increment. Just as in a one-team-Scrum environment, individual Developers don't show local versions of the product that are not integrated, in scaled Scrum individual Scrum Teams don't show local versions of the product that are not integrated.

Sprint Retrospective

The Sprint Retrospectives still take place in scaled Scrum. The idea of scaling the concept of the Sprint Retrospective across individual teams is logical and is therefore found in all scaling frameworks.

Each team should still conduct their own Sprint Retrospectives. The issues identified during these may be taken by a representative to a scaled Sprint Retrospective, which may identify patterns and derive common action items between the Scrum Teams.

Solutions: True, False, True, True, False, False, True, False, True

Metrics and Tools

Question	True	False
Scrum mandates the use of burn-ups and burn-downs.		
Velocity is a perfect predictor of future performance.		
Managers in Scrum environments should create the proper environments for Scrum Teams to thrive.		
Velocity is a useful tool for managers to assess the productivity of a Scrum Team.		
Velocity is not a good indicator for the value generated by the work of a Scrum Team.		

Scrum itself does not prescribe any specific metrics or tools to use. The Scrum Guide mentions burn-downs, burn-ups, and cumulative flow diagrams as being (potentially) useful in measuring progress and forecasting into the near future. These are, however, options and their use is at the discretion of the Scrum Team.

A metric commonly associated with Scrum Teams is "velocity", which usually refers to the number of Product Backlog items finished per Sprint or - if estimations in story points are done - the sum of Story Points of the items finished per Sprint. The Scrum Guide does not mention velocity and its use and exact definition are left up to the individual Scrum Teams. Should such a metric be used, however, there are three important things to keep in mind:

- Velocity is a measure of the past. Extrapolating it into the future is merely a forecast, nothing perfectly reliable. The further into the future any extrapolation is, the less certain you can be about the reliability.
  If a Scrum Team has consistently finished Product Backlog items worth 30 story points each past Sprint, it is a reasonable assumption that roughly the same will be possible in the next Sprint. As we are dealing with complex situations, though, it can also turn out completely differently. Half the Developers might get sick at the same time and the selected items could all turn out much more complicated than expected, leading to only 15 story points worth of items being finished.

- Velocity is an internal metric, not an instrument of management. Managers in Scrum environments should provide support and create the right environment for peak value generation. Therefore, discussing trends in velocity with members of the management can be useful in that it creates transparency to the management about possible impediments or hardships faced by the Scrum Team. Velocity is, however, not a useful metric for managers to evaluate and possibly even control the performance of a Scrum Team.
  Imagine a manager ordering the team to increase the velocity by 10%. If velocity measures the number of items, the team may simply use their refinement to decompose their items further, leading to the same value being generated in the same timeframe but with more Product Backlog items. If velocity measures the number of story points, the Developers may simply increase their estimates, leading to the same value being generated in the same timeframe but with more story points being completed.

- Velocity is not a forecasting tool and not a value metric. Velocity and value have no direct correlation. A Scrum Team might finish 30 Product Backlog items per Sprint, all of which only add marginal new value to their Increment, while another Scrum Team team might finish only 3 Product Backlog items per Sprint, all of which add tremendous value to their Increment. The ultimate goal of the work of the Scrum Team is value generation; velocity can help to better understand the path towards this goal, but cannot replace the goal itself.

Solutions: False, False, True, False, True

Scrum.org Exams

As of January 2021, Scrum.org offers the following certifications:

- Professional Scrum Master (PSM I, II, III)
- Professional Scrum Product Owner (PSPO I, II, III)
- Professional Scrum Developer (PSD I)
- Professional Scrum with User Experience (PSU I)
- Professional Scrum with Kanban (PSK I)
- Scaled Professional Scrum (SPS)
- Professional Agile Leadership (PAL I)
- Professional Agile Leadership - EBM (PAL-EBM)

For most people, the first step into the certifications of Scrum.org is PSM I, which is by far the most rewarded certification, counting over 300,000 certified individuals worldwide. The rarest certifications at this point are the most advanced ones: PSPO III and PSM III.

Lead in Agile provides trainings preparing for all levels of certification, including PSM III, to organizations in English and German. If you are interested, reach our via the contact form on the website: https://lead-in-agile.com

Scrum.org provides practice tests for its exams:

PSM I	Scrum Open
PSPO I	Product Owner Open
PSD I	Scrum Developer Open
PSK I	Scrum with Kanban Open
SPS	Nexus Open
PAL I	Agile Leadership Open
PAL-EBM	Evidence-Based Management Open

Image Sources

- Scrum.org profile of Moritz Knueppel: By Moritz Knueppel – All rights reserved
- Cynefin Framework: Snowden, CC BY 3.0 <https://creativecommons.org/licenses/by/3.0>, via Wikimedia Commons

Disclaimer

The rights to the "Professional Scrum" brand is owned by Scrum.org. All uses of this in its full and abbreviated forms are descriptive and do not imply any association or endorsement of any of the contents in this book by Scrum.org.
All information provided in this book is the author's personal opinion and implies no association or connection with Scrum.org. For the sake of readability, PSM will be used without a trademark sign inside this book.

In the interest of compactness, some aspects described in the book have been simplified, such as describing the Product Owner and Scrum Master as a roles, rather than as an accountabilities filled by people within the Scrum Team.

Sources

[1] 2020 Scrum Guide, page 3, https://scrumguides.org/docs/scrumguide/v2020/2020-Scrum-Guide-US.pdf

[2] https://en.wikipedia.org/wiki/Cynefin_framework

[3] 2020 Scrum Guide, page 5

[4] 2017 Scrum Guide, page 6, https://scrumguides.org/docs/scrumguide/v2017/2017-Scrum-Guide-US.pdf

[5] 2020 Scrum Guide, page 5

[6] 2020 Scrum Guide, page 6

[7] 2017 Scrum Guide, page 6

[8] July 25, 2012 blog post on kenschwaber.wordpress.com, https://kenschwaber.wordpress.com/2012/07/25/self-organization-and-our-belief-that-we-are-in-charge/

[9] https://www.amazon.com/dp/1680501283

[10] https://www.scrum.org/resources/8-stances-scrum-master

[11] 2020 Scrum Guide, page 6

[12] 2020 Scrum Guide, page 6

[13] Bernard. M. Bass: The Bass Handbook of Leadership, Theory, Research & Managerial Applications. 4th edition. New York 2008, p. 1091

[14] 2020 Scrum Guide, page 6

[15] 2020 Scrum Guide, page 5

[16] 2020 Scrum Guide, page 7

[17] 2013 Scrum Guide, page 10, https://scrumguides.org/docs/scrumguide/v1/Scrum-Guide-US.pdf

[18] 2017 Scrum Guide, page 12

[19] 2017 Scrum Guide, page 5

[20] 2020 Scrum Guide, page 10

[21] 2017 Scrum Guide, page 15

[22] 2020 Scrum Guide, page 11

[23] 2020 Scrum Guide, pages 11f.

[24] 2020 Scrum Guide, page 4

[25] 2020 Scrum Guide, page 5